Malinche's CONQUEST

Malinche's CONQUEST

ANNA LANYON

ALLEN & UNWIN

Every effort has been made to contact the copyright holders of material reproduced in this text. In cases where these efforts were unsuccessful, the copyright holders are asked to contact the publisher directly.

This project has been assisted by the Commonwealth Government through the Australia Council, its arts funding and advisory body.

Australia Council for the Arts

First published in 1999 by
Allen & Unwin
83 Alexander Street
Crows Nest NSW 2065
Australia
Phone: (61 2) 8425 0100
Fax: (61 2) 9906 2218
E-mail: frontdesk@allen-unwin.com.au
Web: http://www.allenandunwin.com

National Library of Australia
Cataloguing-in-Publication entry:

Lanyon, Anna.
Malinche's conquest.

Bibliography.
Includes index.
ISBN 1 86448 780 1.

1. Marina, ca. 1505–ca. 1530. 2. Indians of Mexico — Biography.
3. Aztec women — Biography. 4. Mexico — History — Conquest,
1519–1540. I. Title.

972.02

Set in 11 pt Adobe Garamond
Cover and text design by Ruth Grüner
Map on p. xvi by Mike Gorman
Printed by Griffin Press, South Australia

3 5 7 9 10 8 6 4

About the Author

ANNA LANYON studied Spanish, Portuguese and History at La Trobe University in Melbourne. She travelled widely before settling with her family on the southern coast of Victoria, near Portland. She teaches and translates Spanish, and this book is, in part, a consequence of her enduring passion for languages and history. Anna works in Portland for La Trobe University's Centre for the Study of Mothers' and Children's Health, and continues to write whenever she can. She is Honorary Research Fellow with the Institute of Latin American Studies at La Trobe University.

Dedicated to the
memory of Bill Owen
who showed me the house
of Bernal Diaz

Contents

I

prelude

II

conquest

List of Illustrations

*Painting by Jose Clemente Orozco of Cortés and Malinche. Courtesy of Instituto
de Investigaciones Esteticas, UNAM, Mexico (colour photograph). Detail of mural
showing Malinche and son, from Diego Rivera's mural 'La Historia de Mexico'.
Courtesy of Instituto de Investigaciones Esteticas, UNAM, Mexico (colour photograph).
Engraving of Malinche being presented to Cortés at Potonchan. Reproduced with
permission of The Bancroft Library, University of California (p. 59).
The lines from 'Conjectural Poem' by Jorge Luis Borges (p. 2) are taken from* Journey
Through the Labyrinth *by Gerald Martin and are reproduced by permission of Verso.*

Preface

In July 1519 when Hernan Cortés embarked on the momentous adventure we now call the Conquest of Mexico, an Amerindian woman was by his side. She became a witness to, and participant in, the calamitous events that would follow. Cortés knew her as 'Marina'; history remembers her as 'Malinche'.

When I first became interested in this woman I was surprised to find that little reliable biographic data existed for her. I know now that I should not have been surprised. Searching for Malinche I have learned the hard way that she exemplifies a problem defined adroitly by French historians Georges Duby and Michelle Perrot in 1992 in their study *A History of Women: From Ancient Goddesses to Christian Saints*. Duby and Perrot warn that women in the past have left few and tenuous traces for us to follow and examine; that those they have left have not usually originated with themselves anyway, but have come down to us 'filtered through the gaze of the men who held the reins of power, defined official memory, and controlled public archives'.

This has certainly proved to be the case with Malinche.

So why pursue such a difficult undertaking? First because although the woman behind the name 'Malinche' remains an enigma, it has been exciting to retrieve vital fragments of her life, and the story they tell — of survival amid catastrophe — strikes me as both intriguing and poignantly familiar, as we near the end of the twentieth century. Secondly because the evolution and manipulation of her legend demonstrates something of the selective manner in which human societies choose our heroes and villains — editing, excising, simplifying, distorting, for the sake of ideology or national identity. Malinche's story, and what was made of it, can be read as a cautionary tale for all of us.

Readers will find both Spanish and Nahuatl words in this book, along with various spellings of place names and personal names. This apparently chaotic spelling is the natural consequence of Spanish ears recording and approximating as best they could the sounds of a Native American language they had not encountered before. Where these variations occur within direct quotations I have left them intact, in part because it is interesting to see those early stammerings. A glossary of pronunciation at the back of this book will assist with pronunciation so that no one need be left floundering among the exotic sounds of Nahuatl. Also, at the back of the book is a timeline, tracing significant events.

I have incurred many debts in preparing this manuscript. My friend Lesley Jackson encouraged me from the first when the book was still just a few scribbled lines on a page. Chris Koller and Nanette Carter offered me a home and their company in Melbourne when I needed to spend prolonged time in the city for *preface*

research purposes. Professor Inga Clendinnen gave me advice and reassurance at crucial stages along the way. My sister, Louise Wilson, and my friend, Dr Bill Owen, found essential documents and articles for me when I was unable to locate them. Bill's enthusiasm for this work comforted me at difficult moments. I regret very deeply that he did not live to see its completion.

In Mexico, Rosamaria Zuñiga, Filomena Alvarado Ortiz, Luis de Cuesta, Maria Luz Ramirez and Jose Guadalupe Moreno offered me their wisdom as well as their friendship. My family, David, Lucie, Anna and Patrick, showed patience and understanding as they learned to live with Malinche. My parents may have started the whole thing off years ago when they gave me *The Heart of Jade* by Salvador de Madariaga. My thanks go to Bernadette Foley for her sympathetic editing, to Christa Munns and Meridyn Lyle for their patience in guiding me to a safe landing in the final stages, and to Ruth Grüner for endowing this book with such visual beauty. But my deepest gratitude must go to Jackie Yowell, my publisher. Without her constant and unfailing support and encouragement I would have abandoned this project long ago.

Anna Lanyon
Narrawong, May 1999

MEXICO
*Independent Kingdoms
(Various Cultures)*

Gulf of

La Malinche

Mexico City
(Tenochtitlan)   Lake Texcoco   Jalapa
                                      Veracruz
Iztaccihuatl
Popacatepetl   Tlaxcala

                                  Coatzacoalcos
                                  Acayucan
Culhua-Mexica (Aztec)   Jaltipan
Empire AD 1325-1521   Grijalva
                                      Isthmus of
                                      Tehuantepec

Non-Aligned Independent Kingdoms
Former Olmec Heartland 1500-400 BC

Cortés's route from Cuba to Tenochtitlan ___ ___ ___
            1519-1521

Malinche's route from Jaltipan to Potonchan
to Tenochtitlan   c.1510-1521 ·············   Pacific

Malinche and Cortés's final journey from _____
Tenochtitlan to Honduras and back by sea
            1524-1526

Cuba
Conquered by Spain 1492

Mexico

Yucatan Peninsula

Caribbean Sea

Xicalango
Candelaria R.
Potonchan
lla
rmosa
Usumacinta R.
Belize
Lake Peten
Tayasal
(Flores)

Mayan Realms
AD 300-1530s

Honduras

Guatemala

El Salvador

Ocean

Nicaragua

Malinche's CONQUEST

I

prelude

To this sombre evening was I led

by a multiple labyrinth of steps,

woven by my days,

since one day in my childhood.

JORGE LUIS BORGES, *'Conjectural Poem'*

The Absent Figure

In September 1997 I put a telephone call through to Mexico City, to the famous Museo Nacional de Antropologia. The receptionist told me the person I wanted to speak to no longer worked there. She had transferred to another institute in Colima, on the west coast of Mexico. Would I like her number?

I called Colima and waited nervously while the secretary went to find Rosamaria Zuñiga. How would I explain who I was and what I was doing? Would she think I was crazy? I heard the sound of footsteps on a wooden floor, then her voice: '*Bueno?*' I began. I explained that I had tried to find her when I was last in Mexico in 1994. I had wondered about her ever since because I had heard that, like me, she was researching the life and legend of Malinche. That's why I had finally summoned the courage to ring.

I need not have worried. That was the first of many long conversations Rosamaria and I would have, by telephone, by mail. She told me she had moved to Colima, beneath its beautiful volcanoes called 'Fire' and 'Ice', Fuego and Hielo, to escape the pollution and crime of Mexico City.

She was an anthropologist and linguist. As well as her native Spanish she spoke several other European languages and two indigenous Mexican tongues: Zapotec and Nahuatl. I explained that my background was also in language, but I knew only Spanish and Portuguese. As for Nahuatl, it interested me greatly, although I had only a passing knowledge of this beautiful tongue.

On one occasion Rosamaria remarked on the curious nature of our friendship; about how strange it was that we should have been brought together by a woman who had disappeared five hundred years ago. Something else she said about Malinche has stayed with me. She described her as the absent figure always present in the history of the Conquest of Mexico. '*El personaje ausente siempre presente*' were her precise words. Even after all this time I can think of no better definition of Malinche.

Malinche really lived. It is important to say this at the outset because the little that remains of her story is so fragmentary and so elusive as to suggest a mirage, a fantasy. Even in Mexico, where she is remembered with such bitter and enduring poignancy.

It is, as Rosamaria Zuñiga said, almost five hundred years since Malinche was born. Five hundred years, perhaps a little less. It is difficult to be certain because the year of her birth, like almost every other detail of her brief life, has either been forgotten or was never recorded.

We know, however, that when the Spaniards first encountered her in 1519, she was a young woman, possibly about eighteen or nineteen years of age. The same age, in other words, as the extraordinary, catastrophic century into which she had been born.

She was living among the Maya at that time, in a city which no longer exists, on the gulf coast of what we now call Mexico. But she was not a Mayan. Her birthplace lay some 200 kilometres to the west, on a slender land bridge, an isthmus, well outside Mayan territory.

She had learned to speak the Mayan tongue, or more specifically, the branch of Mayan spoken in that remote coastal region at the base of the Yucatan Peninsula. She also knew Nahuatl, which belonged, and still belongs, to an entirely different family of languages from Mayan. In Malinche's day it was spoken by various peoples of central Mexico, including, most famously, the Aztecs. Nahuatl is essential to Malinche's story, because it was the language the Aztecs spoke, and because she retained it throughout her years among the Maya. As if in preparation for what was to come.

I saw Malinche first in Mexico City, on the walls of the Palacio Nacional. She was a solitary woman in Diego Rivera's famous mural; a woman amid a sea of conquistadors and priests, warriors in jaguar skins, ghostly penitents in their pointed hats. She stood there framed within an arch at the base of a great staircase. Her long black hair was swept back from her face. She wore the graceful white cotton tunic, the *huipil*, I had seen worn by the Mayan women of the south, and like them, her only adornments were a pair of earrings and a long string of beads, coiled twice around her neck.

I noticed that she clasped a small boy to her and that the child's face was buried in her dress, in an attitude of fear. Her own expression, as she glanced toward Hernan Cortés, was vigilant. She was surrounded by people but she seemed entirely alone with her child.

I turned to the friend who had brought me to the National Palace.

'Who is she?' I asked him.

'That's Malinche,' he said. 'Have you never heard of her?'

I shook my head, but I didn't take my eyes off the woman.

'She was Cortés's guide,' he said, 'and his interpreter through-out the Conquest.'

'And who is this child with her?'

'That is their son,' he replied. 'I don't recall his name, but he was the first of us.'

'The first Mexican?' I asked him, puzzled.

'Yes,' he said. 'In a way, yes. He was the first child of a Spanish father and an Amerindian mother. The first *mestizo*.'

It was January 1974. Walking outside in the wintry streets of this mountain city I could see my breath, and even inside those thick palace walls, the air was cold. I stood there looking at Malinche and I was moved by her watchful solitude and by her tenderness toward the child in her arms.

In the months that followed I heard her name frequently, or rather, a derivative of her name, *Malinchista*. I noticed that politicians hurled it at each other, like a lightning rod. It sounded to me like a derisive war cry.

'Why do they do that?' I asked my friend. 'What do they mean when they say that word, '*Malinchista*'?

'It is an insult,' he explained. 'It implies that one is not truly

Mexican. That one is too susceptible to foreign influence. A traitor. Like Malinche.'

I listened quietly. I had no argument. I still knew very little of Mexico and almost nothing of this woman's story.

Most mornings I would rise early to watch the twin volcanoes as they loomed above the city, snowcapped, remote, a menacing trail of smoke floating high above the larger of the two. It was still possible, in those days, to glimpse them in the rosy light of dawn, before they disappeared behind their concealment of cloud.

As a child I liked to recite their wondrous, polysyllabic names. '*Popo-cat-epetl*', I would whisper to myself, '*Iztac-cihuatl*'. I even knew what they meant: 'Smoking Mountain', 'White Lady'. Those extravagant, alluring words were my first encounter with Nahuatl, but I mistakenly assumed they were Spanish since that was the official language of Mexico.

I had longed to visit Mexico City. To me it was the eternal city of the Americas. But I hadn't counted on modernity. Who does? My eyes wept caustic tears in the contaminated air and I felt lost in its noise and complexity. I found my way, however, to the secluded plazas of the old quarter, to the leaning palaces and churches, the narrow lanes leading into the great central square they call the Zocalo.

I felt that shock of recognition when you gaze upon a building or a streetscape you have long known from drawings and etchings, from paintings and photographs. Moctezuma's city, Cortés's city. The oldest continually inhabited metropolis in the Americas. This was the Mexico City of my imagination. It did not disappoint me.

I walked each day through the pretty Alameda Central. This peaceful woodland was once the city's official burning place, the *quemadura*, where Jews and heretics had met a fiery death at the hands of their tormentors. I knew this, but still I found it difficult to imagine such horror amid such beauty.

A few blocks away I saw a huge plumed serpent which Aztec hands had carved from stone without ever knowing that their sacred sculpture would one day form the cornerstone of a foreign palace thrust down upon the ruins of their proud city. I sat in a primitive Spanish church that had extinguished an older shrine to an earlier god. In all these places, like everyone who comes to Mexico City, I sensed the ancient pulse of the Amerindian past. But I didn't see Malinche's house that first time, or realise that it stood so close nearby, silent and forgotten beside the Plaza de Santo Domingo.

I no longer recall where I stayed on that first visit to Mexico City. Somewhere in the district of Tacuba, I think, on an upper floor where an unbearable neon sign outside the window disturbed my sleep each night.

At breakfast on the morning of the day I was due to leave, I was leafing through a tattered art book on the shelf in the vestibule, and read about another painting of Malinche in Mexico City.

I asked the concierge for directions, left my bags with her and took a bus to the central plaza. I hurried past the cathedral and along Calle Donceles, determined to see this work before leaving.

In 1923 the old Jesuit College of San Ildefonso became the National Preparatory School, and along its gallery walls Diego

Rivera painted a series of luminous murals. While he was working on them he met Frida Kahlo, who later became his wife. The
College is filled with great art, not only Rivera's but that of his
magnificent rival muralist, Jose Clemente Orozco. It was one of
Orozco's paintings I had come to see: Cortés and Malinche.

I walked quickly through the galleries and halls. I searched
and searched but I couldn't find it. Time was running out when
I finally located an attendant who told me to walk across the
courtyard, up a staircase that I had not noticed, and when I reach
the first landing, turn and look back.

I took the steps leading up from the courtyard and turned as
instructed. I saw her there in the shadows, on the sloping under-
side of the staircase. It was an inspired work which almost leapt
from the grey stone on which it was painted. Orozco's Malinche
wears no ornament. She is naked, sullen and brooding. Her
copper skin glows in the darkness beneath the staircase, but her
eyes are cast down, her arm hangs by her side. She seems barely
conscious, unknowable, hermetic, silent, immense.

Hernan Cortés is there, ghostly pale but unassailable, with his
arm thrust like a barricade across her body. Is he restraining or
protecting her? I couldn't tell. He grasps her hand in his and
glares out at the world, fearless, implacable in his place beside
her. Beneath his feet a vanquished Amerindian warrior lies face
down, his arm raised toward the inert, unseeing Malinche.

Orozco's Malinche is an intensely carnal, disturbing portrait,
and it seemed to me the artist had deliberately concealed it in
that sombre place beneath the stairs. But I was wrong. Later, as
I learned more about the polemical storm which rages forever

around Malinche, I came to understand this painting differently. I saw it as the artist's own defiant, public memorial to this illicit mother of modern Mexico.

That night as I flew out of Mexico City, I farewelled the lights spread out before me and the strange dark patch in their midst which is all that remains of the lake on which the old Aztec capital was originally constructed.

As we flew north across the sierra, I remembered the mural on the walls of the National Palace, and the painting beneath the stairs in the Colegio de San Ildefonso. I went away, but I never forgot about Malinche.

⚜

It was another three years before I returned to Australia. When I did I became a language student. I had acquired a fumbling, hesitant brand of Spanish, but I felt ashamed and desired something better. Besides, like so many others at that time, I had fallen in love with the Latin American poets. 'I would learn Spanish just to be able to read Pablo Neruda and Borges and Mistral and Juana Inez de la Cruz,' I explained to anyone who would listen.

One of my professors in the years that followed liked to remind us of the complexity of the translators' task. It was essential, she said, to preserve, at all costs, the perfect symmetry of sound and meaning for which the poet had struggled, alone, through the long dark nights.

Should translation of poetry even be attempted? she asked. Was it possible? There were times, she told us, when she still wasn't certain. When you love a poet's work, she warned us, it could feel like a betrayal.

'*Traduttore, traditore,*' she would murmur at these moments, with a cautionary smile. 'Translator, traitor . . . Wise words, don't you think?' Each time I heard her say that, my mind would wander from the work before me. I would look out across the treetops of the university, across the lagoon and the geese sheltering in the reeds, and I would think about Malinche.

She too had been a translator, but in far more dangerous circumstances than those I would ever have to face. Was she also a traitor? I wasn't sure what to think. And although I should have been engaged in other pursuits, I began, instead, to search for her.

I presumed I would find a biography of Malinche on the shelves of the university library. I thought it would be easy, but it wasn't. She was usually just a footnote, a paragraph or two at best, in the many great histories of the Spanish Conquest, or sometimes just a puzzling entry in the index: Marina, *see* Malinche. Malinche, *see* Marina.

A woman of several names, of uncertain origins, of unknown purpose. Who was she? Why did she do what she did? Had she betrayed her people, as I had heard in Mexico? Who were her people anyway?

One thing I learned quickly and with extreme regret. Although Malinche was there at all the great moments of the Conquest, although she spoke for Cortés, although the phrases she learned to utter on his behalf were carefully recorded, she left not one word of her own to tell us what she made of the apocalyptic events in which she participated. It is one of the many ironies of her story — that she was famous for her voice, but we never hear her speak.

The little we know of her has come down to us almost entirely through the eyes and ears of one man, a Spaniard, a former conquistador. His name was Bernal Diaz del Castillo. He said he knew Malinche, and the fragmentary glimpses he offered of her in his memoirs of the Conquest became precious to me beyond estimation.

Bernal Diaz was there in 1519 when the Maya gave Malinche to Cortés. He observed her as she travelled with the Spaniards up from the coast, through the highest mountain passes, to the remote Aztec capital, Tenochtitlan, whose soaring pyramids and temples stood then where Mexico City stands today. He noted that after the Conquest she bore a child to Cortés, and that later she was reunited, briefly, with her family in the Isthmus. Diaz told me more about Malinche than any other historian I had read, and his words had the convincing and compelling power of an eyewitness.

In his closing chapters Diaz gave a meticulous account of the fortunes of each of his comrades in arms. This man died of his wounds, he said, and this man lived to a great old age, and this one drowned, and this one died in such and such a battle. Line after fascinating line, his words went on, like an old soldier's roll-call to his dead companions. But about Malinche's fate he said nothing.

In 1988, some years after I completed my studies, I attended a seminar devoted to Mexican history. Discussion arose about

CORTÉS AND MALINCHE

(painting by Jose Clemente Orozco)

DETAIL OF MURAL SHOWING MALINCHE AND SON

(from Diego Rivera's mural 'La Historia de Mexico')

MOCTEZUMA, CORTÉS, MALINCHE AND
GERONIMO DE AGUILAR
*(from frieze beneath statue of Cuauhtemoc,
Paseo de la Reforma, Mexico City)*

the great seventeenth-century poet, Sor Juana Inez de la Cruz, and I was surprised when one of the speakers invoked Malinche's name. It was not a name I had heard much since leaving Mexico.

'It is interesting to compare,' he intoned, 'the admiration for Sor Juana, as opposed to the contempt reserved for the woman called Malinche.' I glanced at the other participants and guessed from their expressions that they had never heard of her.

'Malinche was Hernan Cortés's guide during the Conquest,' he explained, 'and his mistress. These days in Mexico she is considered a national traitor.' He surveyed the puzzled faces in front of him. 'Have you never heard the expression *Malinchista*?' he asked. No, they hadn't, but I had, and I flinched to hear this pejorative word pronounced out loud.

Some days later I spoke to a fellow student from the history faculty. Like me he had an interest in Mexico, so I told him I was thinking of basing some post-graduate research on Malinche.

'Malinche?' he said. 'Why Malinche?' He looked genuinely shocked.

'Well,' I said hesitantly, 'because she had such a profound impact on Mexico.'

'But what an impact.' He shook his head.

'Why not research the life of Sor Juana, or Josefa Ortiz de Dominguez, the independence leader?' he said. 'Why not choose a more edifying subject?'

'Much of women's experience in this world is unedifying,' I told him. 'Besides, it seems to me there is something universal about what happened to Malinche, during her lifetime, after her death. It's not just a Mexican story.'

Mexico City

It was 1994 by the time I returned to Mexico City. The friend who had shown me the mural in the National Palace twenty years earlier had died in the earthquake of 1985, and I knew no one.

I arrived in the early hours of the morning, *la madrugada*, and was startled to find the air so warm and still after the cold autumn nights I had left behind in the Southern Hemisphere. I took a slow cab from the airport into the heart of the city's old quarter. We made our way down ancient lanes, past shuttered doors and empty balconies.

I felt confused and disoriented by the lateness of the hour and the distance I had travelled, but the driver was young and inquisitive. He wanted to know what I was doing in Mexico City, so we talked for a while and his conversation soothed my nerves. He was proud of his city, and he wished me luck as I stepped from his car. He waited while I entered the sombre portal of a hotel which had once, in some remote century, been prelude

a monastery. I had chosen it for its position beside the Biblioteca Nacional where I intended to do some research.

The concierge handed me my key and indicated a grand old marble staircase winding up from the patio to the floor above. Grand, but unstable. I felt it move beneath my feet as I ascended. I found my room off the first landing. A small cell, scrubbed and barren, with a fragile light peering in through the glass-panelled door.

It was a melancholy Friday toward the end of Lent. Not that I would have remembered this, for it was many years since I had taken note of such observances. But in Mexico the religious calendar still carries far more meaning than the solar year.

A magazine on the table in my room gave a list of the processions that would take place in and around the capital during Holy Week. In the suburb of Iztapalapa, for example, a young man had been chosen to represent Jesus in the local passion play. It was a role his father, his grandfather and his great-grandfather had played before him. He said he wanted to acquit himself with honour and humility, just as they had.

I bathed my face in the washbasin and lay down on the clean hard bed, and it startled me, the silence. For months I had prepared myself for noise, here in the centre of the world's most populous city, but its complex, sad old heart was silent throughout that long and wakeful night of my return, and I heard only the impenetrable quiet of the streets below.

In the morning I walked four blocks in the wrong direction before I realised what I had done. I had been away too long. I had to turn and make my way back along those straight narrow

15

streets laid down in the sixteenth century, proceeding more carefully this time, until the sudden great space of the central plaza opened before me, and I stood at its edge with the morning bells ringing in my ears.

I surveyed the dishevelled skyline of crooked shrines and temples all around and beyond the plaza's rim, and saw that while I had been far away in more serene places, the earthquakes had continued their relentless business of tearing and rocking and reordering the city's weird symmetry.

I looked across to the cathedral and was shocked to see that the ground had subsided beneath it, thrusting the great basilica forward, listing and helpless, like some immense sinking galleon. And there was the eerie beauty I had forgotten.

Where I come from on the southern coast of Australia, the sun glows red in summer, through a dense haze of smoke, as the forests burn. In Mexico City the sun glows crimson all year round, through a sinister, polluted sky, and its lurid gleam intensifies the strangeness of this ancient place, with its jumbled layers of antiquity, set high within its fortress of watchful volcanoes.

I stood for some time seeing all this, remembering, while soldiers, intent on their morning ritual, raised the flag in front of the National Palace. As they completed their task, I crossed to the square's north-west corner and walked north along Calle Republica de Brasil toward the Plaza de Santo Domingo.

A colonnade of stone pillars guards the western flank of this smaller plaza, and within its shade printers were preparing for their day's work. Some were deep in conversation, and, as I stood to catch my breath, I overheard a little of what they were saying. About the crisis down south among the Mayans of Chiapas, about the coming presidential election in August. They were still talking gravely as I turned to the house I had come so far to see.

Number 96, Republica de Cuba is painted a dusky, warm yellow. Its balconies look out toward the shadowy cloisters of the plaza, and it is very old. It was one of the first Spanish houses to rise among the ruins of the Aztec city, and, according to tradition, Malinche had lived here toward the end of her life. The house has known many lives since then. It is now a primary school. That morning, as I stood there, not a sound came from inside, and its massive sixteenth-century doors were firmly closed against me.

I realised it was Saturday. When you are an outsider, it is easy to forget the commonplace routine of other people's lives. I stood looking up at the balconies, but sensing people watching me, I hesitated, not wishing to offend with my interest in this house of a traitor. But I wanted very badly to go inside, to see if some small echo of Malinche still rang within those walls.

The following Monday I joined the mothers waiting for their children in the plaza outside Malinche's house. I felt their glances as I stood among them. Finally the bolt was pulled back, and the massive doors swung open. Lined up before me in the portal were the students, girls in blue dresses with white collars and pinafores, boys in blue shirts and grey trousers. They watched me as I stepped inside.

To the left, where the gatekeeper must once have sat, was a small office. A tall man stood at the only desk in the room, intent on a bundle of papers before him. I asked him if I could walk about in this house that had once been Malinche's. He was the principal, it turned out, and he assented gracefully.

I wondered if he was used to such requests, but he shook his head. No, he said, no one ever came here to look for Malinche, and in any case, very little remained from her time, as I would see. Only the kitchen, which was up the staircase and to the left. He walked with me to the doorway and showed me what he meant. That room alone, he said, pointing toward the floor above us, was more or less untouched. I thanked him, turned and slipped through the children playing outside his office, into the courtyard.

In Mexico City the streets and lanes of the old quarter are full of gracious patios. You glimpse them through open doorways, elegant havens of tranquillity undisturbed since the sixteenth and seventeenth centuries, when they were translated across the ocean from Cordoba and Granada.

The principal had been right to prepare me for disappointment in the case of this building, however. From the street it still looked much as it had in Malinche's day, but inside it had been gutted. It was a workaday school, had been so for many years. My heart sank as I stood in the courtyard whose flagstones had been concreted over, surrounded by cement-sheet partition walls. I felt in its obliterated interior that I would never find anything of Malinche.

At the base of the staircase leading up to the balcony, I saw a small woman watching me. 'Can I assist you, *señora*?' she called to me. She smiled as I approached. Her black hair was pulled back from her forehead in a tidy bun, her face was plump and burnished. She wore a blue cotton dress, and I noticed how worn her shoes were. I explained why I had come, and she welcomed me. She was the grade four teacher. Her students clustered around us as we spoke.

She confirmed what the principal had told me, as she led me upstairs to the kitchen. 'Nothing in here has changed,' she said as she opened the door. 'As far as we can tell it is still more or less as it was in Malinche's day.'

It was a bare and primitive room, ill lit, a place for servants only. I ran my hand along the top of the fireplace where pots had once hung, and crouched at the hearth where meals had been prepared so long ago. It was a storeroom now, too small for any other purpose, and painted a sickly blue, but the teacher was right; little else in this room appeared to have changed. Its impossible dimensions and awkward position had probably protected it, for there was really no way it could easily be incorporated into the main school building.

I thought about Malinche's days within these walls. As I knelt there in that unhappy space, surrounded by these silent, attentive children, I doubted she had ever been truly mistress of this house.

When we left the room, one of the students asked her teacher what I was doing in the school. I have come because of Malinche, I explained. The little girl looked directly at me for the first time. 'I have heard her,' she told me in a firm little voice. 'I have heard her weeping as she walks along the balcony and through the rooms.' The boy beside her nodded eagerly.

'So have I,' he said breathlessly, and I looked from one to the other, moved by their excitement.

I wanted to ask them more, but I could see that their teacher disapproved of their impious enthusiasm for this hapless ghost. 'Señora,' she said, turning to me, 'I have worked here twenty-five years. I have spent hundreds of hours alone here, even at night, and never have I heard this woman. It's superstition, nothing more.' She was a sensible, intelligent woman, and in the face of her exasperation I thought it better to restrain my curiosity.

We left the old kitchen and stumbled along with the children through the shell of Malinche's house, into the grade four classroom. The teacher and I sat down with her students around us, and as they listened, I asked her what she thought about Malinche. I knew that for better or for worse Mexicans loved to talk about her.

She sat erect in her chair and thought for a moment before she spoke. 'Well,' she began, 'many people say she was a traitor. You probably know this.' I nodded. 'But working here in her house . . .' The children were listening intently. 'Well, to me she was just a woman, nothing more.' The teacher shot a stern glance toward her students. 'Just a woman, like you and me. She was dealt a bad hand in life, but she made the best of it. She must have been very young, you know, when she was with Cortés, and then she came here, to this house, to end her days.'

So Malinche might once have walked and talked in this worn old room. I looked around at its bare floor, its clutter of chairs and desks, these bright-eyed children. I went over to the balcony window and glanced out across the plaza toward the beautiful

Iglesia de Santo Domingo. It had not yet been constructed in those early days when she lived here. If she had looked from this balcony in 1526 she would have seen little but the rubble of Aztec temples.

I turned back to the teacher. 'Have you ever heard anything about how or when she might have died?'

'No, nothing I'm afraid,' she replied. 'It's so long ago now. I don't think anybody knows for certain what happened to her.'

She joined me at the window and we stood there in silence.

I told the teacher that I intended going south, to the Isthmus, to where Malinche's life had begun. 'I've never been that far,' she said with wonder. 'It's another world down there.'

'Well, I passed that way once,' I told her, 'during my first visit to Mexico. But I took no notice of the Isthmus then. I didn't understand, you see, about its connection with Malinche. So now I have to go back, retrace my steps.'

The children had lost interest in us. They were playing a game at the blackboard, but its surface was in such disrepair that their broken sticks of chalk made hardly any impression. The teacher told them to stay put while she went out with me. We walked back along the inner balcony, down the stairs, past the old kitchen, to the office beside the front door. She opened the filing cabinet and searched through the folders.

'Yes, here it is.'

She offered me a single sheet of paper, the school's own history of Malinche.

'You take this,' she said, 'we have other copies.'

In the still afternoon heat, in a small dark cafe near the corner of Palma and Tacuba streets, with the dome of the leaning cathedral just in sight, I stopped for coffee. The children's story had not entirely surprised me, for I knew their phantom had a long and melancholy history in Mexico, that she is said to walk the streets of the old quarter, sobbing and lamenting for her children, that some people call her *La Llorona*, the 'Weeping Woman'. But others, like those school children, said she was Malinche.

⚜

Two days later a thick brown cloud of dust descended on the city. I returned to my hotel in the afternoon feeling ill, my face alight with fever, and slept for several hours.

I awoke in the early evening and searched in my diary for a number I had promised to ring. I picked up the telephone beside the bed and dialled. Finally a voice answered, and I asked to speak to Filomena Alvarado. As I waited I heard the clatter of china, the murmur of distant conversation. 'Filomena Alvarado here,' said an elegant voice.

I introduced myself, explained that I had brought gifts from her sister in Australia, and she exclaimed with surprise. 'Could we meet tonight?' she asked. We made a time, a place.

I replaced the receiver and lay back on the pillow, listening to the deep rumble of a jet as it passed low overhead. I had walked too fast through the streets that day, without thought for the altitude, the suffocating air, the sun.

Later that evening I took some aspirin with a glass of purified water and walked the two blocks from my hotel to the address

Filomena had given me. A warm breeze blew across the plaza, the cathedral glowed in the darkness. In the middle of the square a group of Mayans sat huddled in their tent embassy, maintaining their vigil for land rights as they had done for months. They would not return to the jungles of Chiapas, their signs declared, until they had achieved their purpose. Apart from their silent presence the streets seemed deserted.

I found the address I wanted, an old narrow doorway in Donceles, not far from the cathedral. I knocked and within a few minutes a woman opened the door. Filomena Alvarado shared her sister's features: the same large and luminous eyes, the same thin, expressive face. As I got to know her, I noticed how her face could change from severity to laughter without warning. She ushered me into a small sitting room where several other women sat in silence, staring at the television in the corner.

'Have you heard?' she asked me, pointing toward the screen. A reporter stood in a hospital corridor somewhere, speaking urgently into her microphone about a shooting earlier that day.

'It's the presidential candidate,' Filomena whispered. 'Colosio.' He had died that afternoon, she told me, in a hail of bullets, in Tijuana, on the United States border. We watched the footage of his shooting earlier that day, amid a crush of admirers, at point blank range. We saw the blood as they ran toward the ambulance with his supine body. As we watched the television, outside in the streets and plazas the city's silent, desperate grief began.

Political assassinations are rare in Mexico. This was the first in over sixty years. 'I did not admire Colosio,' Filomena told me. 'I would never have voted for him. But this is the kind of madness we associate with the United States. They have had so many such killings, here we have had so few.'

We listened late into the night as Mexico's most eminent commentators came forward to offer their opinions on this anguished moment in their country's history. In the end I felt too desolate to go back, alone, to my hotel, so Filomena made up a bed for me down the hall from her own room. I fell asleep near dawn, as the bells began to toll across the plaza and unseen hands scrawled a poignant message across every wall in the capital: *Mexico repudia la violencia.*

Isthmus

I used to stare at the map of Mexico. I used to trace its strange, explosive shape with my finger and consider what it most resembled: a funnel of smoke, a menacing tornado, even a distorted hourglass twisted on its side. If I ran my finger down along its winding contours, I came to a slender waist, an Isthmus, separating the mountains and deserts of the north from the lagoons and rainforests of the south. This, the atlas told me, was the Isthmus of Tehuantepec.

Human civilisation goes back a long way on this narrow little neck of land. Over a millennium before the time of Christ, the first great temples and pyramids of Meso America were constructed by the Olmec people on its palm-sprinkled plains. Long after the Olmec had vanished, the memory of their grandeur inspired a procession of other dazzling cultures — the Maya, the Mixtec, the Zapotec, the Toltec, the Totonac — through-out the length and breadth, the rainforests and mountains of Meso America.

But the last and most short lived of those great civilisations, the Aztec, never held sway in the Isthmus. This low-lying delta of terrible heat and ferociously independent kingdoms marked the limits of Aztec hegemony in sixteenth-century Mexico, just as the Pyrenees once formed a natural barrier between Islamic Spain and Christian Europe.

Following his capture, the emperor, Moctezuma, explained all this to Cortés. He said that his dominion did not extend to the Isthmus, and Cortés relayed this information to the King of Spain in his next despatch. 'The people of this province,' Cortés wrote, 'are not vassals or subjects of Mutezuma [*sic*]; rather his enemies.'

The Isthmus was the cradle of Mexican civilisation, and it was also the place where Malinche's life began. The guidebooks will tell you she was an Aztec princess. But they are wrong. She came from somewhere out there on the Isthmus, among the remnants of those Olmec temples, among the marshes and estuaries of this ancient tendril of land, where the alluvial plains sweep away toward the warm, still waters of the Gulf.

The places I was looking for had resonant, elusive names: Potonchan, Xicalango, Paynala, Jaltipan, Olutla, Texixtepec. The first three no longer exist and have virtually slipped from memory, while the last three are tiny, archaic and very little known, even within the Isthmus. But each of them is connected in some way to Malinche's story.

Hernan Cortés said she came from 'Putunchan'. 'My interpreter,' he told the King of Spain in a letter of October 1520, 'is an Indian woman from Putunchan.' He meant

Potonchan. It was the Mayan town on the eastern side of the Isthmus, where he found her in 1519.

But the evidence, fragmentary as it is, suggests that Malinche's actual birthplace was somewhere much nearer the centre of the Isthmus. Many years after Malinche's death a number of old conquistadors testified, in a property dispute initiated by her daughter, that they had heard she came originally from either Olutla or Texixtepec. Malinche's grandson never knew her, but he claimed, in a separate legal action of 1604, that she had been born in a place called Jaltipan.

Olutla, Texixtepec, Jaltipan. These are places of interest only to the specialist, or the eccentric. All three are neighbouring villages that huddle together in a tight little cluster close to the present-day gulf port of Coatzocoalcos. All three must be considered possibilities.

Bernal Diaz del Castillo, the soldier–historian, had a fourth proposition and unlike the others, his was not based solely on hearsay. He said Malinche had told him that she came from a town called Paynala, which then stood about eight leagues from Coatzocoalcos, and had other villages subject to it. Eight leagues would be about 40 kilometres. But there is no longer any village of this name in the region, much less within that radius from Coatzocoalcos.

Searching for Malinche's origins, I used to fear that I would never find a path through this tangle of conflicting claims about her birthplace, but eventually, sorting through maps and monographs, I came across a possible solution. There is a story, still current in the district around Coatzocoalcos, that sometime late in the sixteenth century the people of Jaltipan fled their ancient site on the banks of the Coatzocoalcos River to escape the ravages of pirates who had penetrated upstream from the coast. The refugees from Jaltipan are said to have fled to a place called Paynala.

It is a fragile clue, based solely on oral tradition, but not implausible. It offers a feasible explanation for the disappearance of Paynala, as its identity was gradually subsumed by the newcomers from Jaltipan, and it allows us to reconcile at least two of these accounts, that of Malinche's grandson and that of Bernal Diaz. As for Olutla and Texixtepec, those villages mentioned by the witnesses in the 1542 property dispute, they may well have been the subject towns to which Bernal Diaz referred.

Whatever the truth of this matter, one thing is certain, of this trio of obscure villages, Jaltipan has always held the strongest and most steadfast claim to being Malinche's birthplace. That was why I wanted so much to go there.

Jaltipan lies sweltering in a delta of crushing heat, in the narrowest part of the Isthmus, just south of the port of Coatzocoalcos. I went early to avoid the heat, but the women in the marketplace had come earlier, at dawn, with their chillis and tomatoes and their purple ears of corn, and their sad bundles of live iguanas, forelegs tied with string behind their backs.

One of the iguana sellers caught my eye with a mocking glint. 'We eat them, you know,' she said, nodding toward the captive lizards.

prelude

'I know,' I replied, 'and you eat armadillos too, don't you?'
'No,' she replied. 'We ate all of them!'

She was small and elegant, with her gleaming black braids and her elaborate blouse, and she rocked with laughter at my dismay. But I was a novelty and she wanted to talk.

She told me she came to Jaltipan on market days but her home was nearer Texixtepec. She wanted to know what I was doing in the village, and I told her I had come because of Malinche. 'Well,' she said, 'this is Malinche's country, for certain.'

She asked me if I knew about Tacamichapa, but I didn't understand what she meant.

'Tacamichapa,' she said. 'It's a floating island down the Chiquito,' and she gestured toward the south, in the direction of the river. She bent down and with a stick drew a rudimentary map in the dirt at our feet.

What she wanted to tell me about Tacamichapa was this. After the Conquest Hernan Cortés had given the floating island to Malinche as a present; a swamp with no solid ground on which to walk, where nothing grew but serpents and mosquitoes. A cruel present, laden with contempt, or just a bitter local joke? I didn't know what to make of her story, but the iguana seller told me it was what she had heard.

The marketplace was bustling with people now and she had work to do. While she attended to a customer, I watched a tiny hummingbird hover against the wall behind her, its wings an invisible blur as it drank deep from a cascade of honeysuckle. When she had finished I asked her to tell me what she thought about Malinche.

'In Mexico City,' I said, 'some people say she was a traitor.'

'*La capital?*' she sniffed dismissively. 'It's a different world up there.' But she considered my question.

'Well, they say that she was beautiful,' she said, '*muy, muy hermosa*, and clever too.' She hesitated for a moment, she was thinking. 'But perhaps not clever enough . . . if all she got for her trouble was Tacamichapa.' And she smiled her sardonic smile.

'Do you know what happened to her in the end?' I asked. It was my constant question, an absurd question, one to which I never really expected an answer but felt compelled to ask. I was searching for the smallest glimmer of possibility, or imagination.

'Who knows?' the iguana seller replied. 'Maybe she ended up beneath that mound of dirt, beside the municipal palace, like people say. But sometimes we hear her in the night. We hear her coming along the river.'

'What do you hear?' I asked.

She was methodically erecting a pyramid of miniature tomatoes on the straw mat before her, but she paused and looked up at me with a puzzled expression, as if I should have known. And I did know, even before the words had left her mouth.

'We hear her weeping for her children,' she replied.

There were ancient silk-cotton trees in the plaza at Jaltipan, and a dirt road leading off toward the edge of the village. The earth was soft beneath my feet as I followed the path, but not far beyond the thrifty cottages and tiny corn patches it came to a sudden end in the shadows of a dark green canopy of trees. I noticed that this little street was called La Calle de la Malinche. It had been named for her.

Beside the municipal palace was the burial mound where, according to local legend, Malinche lies buried. It was less than two metres high, just a hummock of grass-covered earth, like a bronze-age barrow, with who knows what beneath it. Perhaps some forgotten remnant of the Olmec era, perhaps nothing whatsoever.

In Mexico, especially in the south, such mounds are commonplace. Sometimes, beneath their tangle of earth and vine they conceal the remains of temples and pyramids, but most will never be excavated. Only an infinite amount of money and intensive labour would make it possible.

An old man was sweeping the pavement outside the municipal palace. He assured me it was true that Malinche was entombed there. After Cortés abandoned her, the old man told me earnestly as he leant on his broom, Malinche had made her way back here, because this is where she was born and where she wished to die.

In the months that followed no one I talked to in the field of Mexican archaeology gave any credence to the story that this mound was Malinche's burial place. But in Jaltipan, despite what the experts might say, the legend endures, like the memory of Malinche herself.

I walked slowly back toward the silk-cotton trees in the plaza, and sat down in their abundant shade to contemplate this place that still claims Malinche as its own. I saw how clean the buildings were, how artless and new: the concrete square in which I sat, the ungainly church across the street, the municipal palace. Jaltipan has demolished all evidence of its past, but beneath its dull mantle of modernity it is an ancient place. The Olmec ruins of San Lorenzo are only 30 kilometres away. The village has endured throughout the centuries, here in the midst of the Olmec heartland.

Malinche's story is a Mexican story, and yet to make sense of her tumultuous life, it is necessary to forget present-day Mexico. It did not exist, neither in name, nor as a national entity, at the dawn of the sixteenth century, when she was born. If she came back tomorrow she would not recognise it, for the old political and cultural divisions that shaped her life have long been extinguished. The Mexico I saw in 1994 was fashioned by European hands to accord with European concepts and desires.

So what was Jaltipan's place in the pre-Conquest world, before the Spanish came? We have it on the authority of Moctezuma himself that it did not belong to the Aztec empire. We also know that it was too far west to be included in the realm of the Maya. All things considered, it was probably a small, independent principality, like other Isthmus towns at that time. But who were Jaltipan's people, Malinche's people?

The truth about Jaltipan's cultural identity lies buried beneath the weight of Spanish colonial policy. After the Conquest, when Spain set about dividing Mexico into neat provincial segments, it did so according to its own needs, regardless of traditional cultural and political boundaries. This has left us with a dilemma familiar to students of Australian and African history: how to make sense of the indigenous past when its complexity has been flattened and, in some cases, obliterated, beneath a European template.

Linguistic maps, however, can tell us things a map concerned exclusively with geography cannot. Linguistic maps with their neat little patches of texture and geometric pattern speak of cultures and languages overlain by empires, of populations displaced in the throes of conquest, of small, surprising pockets of unexpected languages. Malinche, for example, is usually assumed to have come from Jaltipan and to have been a native speaker of Nahuatl. Therefore it is curious to learn that according to the linguistic maps Nahuatl is not native to the Jaltipan district.

There is no doubt that Nahuatl speakers had begun drifting across from the west by the time Malinche was born. They had brought their language with them, driving what anthropologists call a 'Nahuatl wedge' into this old Olmec territory. But it is also clear that the villagers of Jaltipan still spoke their own tongue and clung to it, even when the intruders coined a contemptuous name for it: *Popoluca*. It means 'babble' in Nahuatl. The babble of foreigners, a barbaric tongue.

These days only the name those intruders gave that ancient language has survived, as if to remind us of the disdain with which they perceived their new home in the centre of the Isthmus. Popoluca, as they called it, had no status in the immigrants' eyes, but its roots in the Isthmus are old indeed. It is a member of the Zoque group of languages. It may once have been the language of the Olmec. Was it also Malinche's mother tongue? Did she acquire Nahuatl as a second language, either in Jaltipan, or later, in one of the places she passed through?

These are not just idle questions. If we knew the answers we would understand something of Malinche's cultural identity. They might tell us, for example, whether she belonged to the newly arrived immigrants from the west, or to a traditional Isthmus family. But Bernal Diaz does not mention Popoluca when he describes Malinche's linguistic abilities.

This is not surprising. Searching for Malinche, we see only what men like Bernal Diaz see, hear only what they hear, read only what they choose to record. No matter how many Amerindian tongues Malinche may have spoken, only Nahuatl was important to Diaz. Therefore only Nahuatl would have been considered worth noting in his memoirs.

It was still early when I saw Luis de Cuesta coming toward me across the plaza. He sat down beside me on the stone bench. 'So,' he said in his quiet voice, 'you have finally seen Jaltipan.'

I had met Luis the previous day, in neighbouring Acayucan, where he worked as a tourist officer. It was he who had alerted me to the story about Paynala and Jaltipan. Like me he was an outsider in the Isthmus, and like me he had an interest in Malinche. We had agreed to meet here in the plaza because he wanted to show me her garden.

'Do you see those trees?' he asked, pointing to a dusky halo of leaves just visible behind the municipal palace. 'That is it.'

We stepped out into the blinding heat and walked toward the burial mound. Passing through a dense wall of greenery behind it, we entered a dappled, limpid world of viridescent saplings, of silk-cotton trees, of arching figs, zapotes, palms. The garden was only a few metres from the roadside but there were no signs to point the way, it was entirely hidden and anonymous. Without Luis I never would have found it.

The point at which we stood was at the same level as the street behind us, but then the ground dropped suddenly away to a lower level, to a rectangle almost the size of the ancient ball-courts you see in the Mayan ceremonial sites further south. We walked carefully down a set of stone stairs to that second level, and while the drone of insects engulfed us, we stood looking up and around at the old stone walls of Malinche's garden.

The grass beneath our feet was carefully mown, stone seats lined the perimeter, a stone aqueduct decended from street level. The garden would have made a fine refuge from the suffocating heat of these parts, but Luis said the villagers did not seem to use this place, although they maintained it with great care. No one ever came here, he told me. They preferred the bright visibility of the streets above.

'Can it ever really have been hers?' I asked him.

'I don't believe so,' he replied. 'Well, not in its present form. It was not laid down until early in the eighteenth century.'

'So,' I said, thinking, 'two hundred years after her death.'

He nodded. 'But I am convinced it must reflect something of her, some lingering remembrance of her life here.'

When I asked Luis to tell me what he knew about Malinche, he recounted the traditional story I had heard so often, while lorikeets shuffled along the branches above our heads. He talked about her childhood in exile among the Maya, about her beauty and courage, her liaison with Hernan Cortés, the way she had led the Spaniards to Moctezuma, had caused the downfall of the Aztec empire.

He reached out to touch the smooth trunk of the palm tree above us. 'It's strange,' he said, 'until I came to live in this district I never thought of her as a real woman. She was more, you know, like a phantom.' He had told me the day before that his home was in the neighbouring state of Chiapas, that he himself was of Mayan ancestry. This was evident in his oval face, his hawk nose, his dark eyes.

'But here, she is so real. Even if she is a prodigal daughter.'

We sat there, in silence, for some time.

'Do you know about the Malinche dances?' he asked me. I told him I did.

'When I was a child,' he said, 'we used to perform one every year in our village in Chiapas. I thought it was just our custom, I had no idea how widespread the dances had become.'

'Yes,' I replied, 'throughout Mexico, in places where Malinche never went, was never seen, in all her lifetime. Even as far north as Arizona. Word of her must have reached every corner, must have penetrated every village and town from north to south.'

I asked him to tell me about the Malinche dance, here in this district of the Isthmus.

'Well the people around here perform it every year, with the other villagers from Olutla, Texixtepec, Sayula de Aleman. They prepare for weeks and weeks — the costumes, the flowers — and then, on the feast day of Mary Magdalene, they begin.'

'Mary Magdalene,' I said. 'How fitting.'

'Yes,' he said, nodding slowly, 'so very appropriate for such a woman. But in the Malinche dance in these parts she is not a villain as she is in some other places. She is more like a prophet, a seer. Her role is to warn Moctezuma of what is coming. She foretells his doom but she is not herself the agent of his destruction.'

'It is quite a different interpretation of her role,' I said.

'Yes. But apart from the dance and these memories, these shadows, there is no tangible evidence of her in Jaltipan anymore, as you can see.'

'It is like that throughout Mexico,' I told him. 'Searching for Malinche . . . it's like pursuing an invisible woman, following a ghost trail. Everyone knows her name, but no one knows who she really was.'

A small black lizard stood balanced, rigid, on the edge of the aqueduct. 'But, even so, the fact that these memories, these unofficial stories, have endured . . . to me that's important in itself.'

He nodded. 'Yes, and you will find, I think, that there is a great difference between the official and the unofficial version of Malinche.' His words were to echo often in my ears, throughout the days and nights ahead.

We walked slowly back toward the eastern end of Malinche's garden and found the mossy steps leading up to street level, and out into the dazzling light above us. I told Luis I would look for him later that day, back in Acayucan.

Suddenly I remembered something. 'Luis, is it still possible to hear Popoluca spoken here in Jaltipan?'

He paused and shook his head.

'As far as I know only a few hundred speakers remain,' he said. 'Around Olutla and Texixtepec. No one knows Popoluca in Jaltipan anymore. There are classes from time to time in the cultural centre in Acayucan, but, to be honest, I think Popoluca is doomed now. Too few speakers and they are all old people.'

I nodded and waved as he walked across the street to the church. Then I returned to the shade of the plaza where I sat for almost an hour, in the centre of that quiet village, poring over my map of the Isthmus, drinking every last drop of water in my flask.

Bernal Diaz writes in his memoirs that Malinche was just a young child when she left Jaltipan. How young he does not say. But he says she told him that she was taken from her home in the Isthmus by 'the men from Xicalango'.

Xicalango. It was once a great trade enclave on the gulf coast, at the base of the Yucatan Peninsula. It was cosmopolitan, famous for attracting merchants from as far south as present-day Honduras and El Salvador, and as far north as the Aztec capital, Tenochtitlan. The fact that Malinche identified these merchants as 'the men from Xicalango' tells us little about their cultural identity. Whoever they were, they carried her east with them, as far as Xicalango, and there she would have seen the famous trade enclave for the first time, nestled along the sheltered banks of a great lagoon, with its huge stone warehouses and wooden jetties.

We do not know how long she spent there. It may have been a matter of days, or weeks, perhaps longer. At some point she was probably sold again, to an anonymous purchaser who carried her further down the gulf coast to Potonchan, a Mayan town, where she began a new life as a child alone and enslaved in a foreign city whose language she could not speak.

Little is known about her time in Potonchan, but some years later, when Hernan Cortés was gathering information about that city, he was told that before the Conquest it had many wealthy lords who kept numerous wives and concubines. If that was true, it seems probable that Malinche spent her early years in the household of one of these rich burghers, learning to weave the beautiful textiles for which the region was famous, until at an appropriate age, perhaps around fourteen, she entered into concubinage.

As far as we can tell, she never spoke about her lost years among the Maya, or if she did her words have not survived. But in Potonchan she grew to adulthood and learned to speak the Mayan tongue, and she was there when the Spaniards arrived in 1519. That was how she became caught up in their invasion.

Bernal Diaz believed that Malinche was a child of provincial nobility in the Isthmus. 'A mistress of vassals' he called her. He also believed that Malinche's own mother had sold her to the men from Xicalango, to ensure that her son, whom she favoured, would inherit the estates and titles that were rightfully Malinche's. It was an elaborate plot, according to Diaz, involving the murder and burial of a young household slave, and the pretence that Malinche herself had died. As the village was lamenting her death, however, she was on her way to Xicalango.

Bernal Diaz said Malinche told him this story herself, and it moved him with its poignant biblical cadence. It made him think of Joseph in the Book of Genesis, when his brothers sold him into slavery among the Egyptians. But what are we to make of it now, five hundred years after the event? How should we interpret this grievous episode in Malinche's early life?

To sell a child, one's own child, seems a profoundly deviant act, unthinkable, unimaginable, yet we know it happens still in parts of the world. We know that families sell their children into prostitution, to pornographers, into factories, into arranged marriages.

Malinche's story is as tragically plausible in the context of her sixteenth-century Amerindian world as it is in ours. We know that it was not uncommon in her time and in her place for children to be sold for the purposes of slavery or sacrifice. We also know that many Meso American cultures at that time had polygamous family structures, and that the children most likely to be sold were the expendable offspring of secondary wives and concubines.

It is possible Malinche's mother was a woman of lowly rank whose status in the family hierarchy prevented her from protecting her child from the whims of her overlord. Or she may have been, as Diaz believed, a provincial noblewoman so ruthlessly ambitious for her son that she would sell her own daughter to slave traders in order to be rid of her.

We know only that in 1525 when this curious woman was reunited briefly with Malinche, she was known as 'Marta'. Like her daughter she had lost her Amerindian name to the new religion. We also know that when Marta came to meet Malinche for that fleeting reunion, her son came with her, and that he was now called 'Lázaro'. But no other information has come to light about this woman to explain or clarify her behaviour toward her daughter.

Bernal Diaz tells us that after the Conquest he became well acquainted with Lázaro. He refers to him as a local *cacique*, or chieftan, in the Coatzocoalcos district, and this lends weight to his claim that Malinche was the child of a noble family. It is also one of few moments in Malinche's story when we have a sense of her in flesh and blood terms — to know that she indeed had a brother, and that Bernal Diaz knew him.

Whatever doubts we may entertain about the motivations behind this painful tale of dynastic conspiracy and disinheritance, Diaz had none. Forty years later when he sat down to record what he remembered of Malinche, he was emphatic about the veracity of his story. 'What I have recorded here,' he wrote, 'I know for certain and can swear to.'

There is another story. Where Malinche is concerned there is always another story. In this instance it is the rumour that her family abandoned her because of her name. Bernal Diaz does not refer to it, perhaps had never heard of it, but it surfaces from time to time. Like the speculation about Paynala and Jaltipan, it belongs to the realm of oral tradition and to the Amerindian side of her legend.

Her original name, according to this interpretation, was Malinalli. It was the name of the twelfth day of the Aztec calendar. It alluded to a blade of grass that could be twisted on the thigh to form a point sharp enough to pierce the tongue, in an act of penance. It was the kind of auto-sacrifice you still see depicted on friezes in the Mayan temples of the south.

Forty years after the Conquest a team of young Aztec scholars working under the guidance of the great Franciscan ethnologist, Bernardino de Sahagun, began the task of recording their peoples' history and culture in a series of famous books known collectively as the Florentine Codex.

These early anthropologists recorded everything they knew in encyclopaedic detail and in their own language, Nahuatl, transposed into the Roman script. They included a lengthy section on the naming of children, and in it they described the name 'Malinalli' as 'like a wild beast'. They said that those born beneath its sign would be difficult, unlucky, rebellious, most terrible of all, their children would be torn away from them.

It was an unenviable destiny, and in retrospect it reads like a portrait of Malinche. In her lifetime she was all of these things, and more. Even the final part of this curse would ring bitterly true for her. But can 'Malinalli', with all its terrifyingly appropriate connotations, seriously have been Malinche's original name? I am alert to the allegorical beauty of this story, with all that it implies about fortune and destiny, but I have never been quite persuaded.

It is true that before the coming of the Spaniards, many cultures in Meso America placed great store in the metaphysical power of names. To them the naming of children was never a simple or arbitrary matter. It was a task entrusted exclusively to priests learned in the workings of the ritual calendars. For all we know Malinche did drag the ill-starred name Malinalli through her childhood years, like a sorrowful amulet, and perhaps it does explain why her family abandoned her.

But this fragment of her story did not arise until many years after her death, far from her birthplace, among people who had never known her, and it is probably more apocryphal than factual, a story constructed in the aftermath of the Conquest. Malinalli, with its forlorn semantic burden and its phonetic resemblance to her Spanish name, Marina, must have seemed painfully appropriate for such a woman.

In the end, these two distinct and melancholy explanations for Malinche's abandonment by her family are all we have: Diaz's story, and the legend of the name. Each in its own way may well have been true, neither can be positively excluded, both belong to the eternally ambiguous narrative of her life.

It was after eleven when a procession emerged slowly and silently from the church in Jaltipan. I closed my notebook as two men placed a small flowered coffin on the tray of a utility truck, and for a moment I thought I glimpsed Luis among the crowd. The mourners raised the banner of Our Lady of Guadalupe above them, and the vehicle moved forward. They began to walk, heads bowed, lips parting softly in prayer, as the child's funeral made its way down the main street toward the village cemetery.

Far away in the north, in his home state of Sonora, the murdered presidential candidate had been buried with much ceremony. In Mexico City the recriminations had begun, amid unseemly jostling for a new presidential candidate. But all the

vain contrivances of the politicians seemed slight and incon-
sequential that morning in remote Jaltipan.

I thought about Malinche's childhood journey from this place,
into slavery among the Maya. No eyewitness account of her
departure has survived, but if anyone watched her go, perhaps her
mother, perhaps a devoted family slave, they would have seen a
slow cortege leaving Jaltipan, led by sumptuously dressed
merchants clasping handsome black staves, the emblem of their
profession. A line of servants follows behind these important
men, carrying textiles, copper tools, dyed rabbit fur, jade and
turquoise in bundles on their backs. Between the bearers and the
merchants walks a small girl. She may not be the only child
among the merchants' precious cargo, but she is unique because
one day she will be remembered as Malinche. Does she hang her
head, or hold it high? Are her hands tied, or is the terror of her
situation enough to restrain her? What does she think about
during her passage into exile? Does she long for the mother she
believes has willingly relinquished her?

I stood up and collected my things, then walked around the
shady footpath to the other side of the marketplace where I
waited for a bus to take me out of Jaltipan.

Exile

I spent the night in the neighbouring city of Acayucan, but I did not stay long, despite its ugly charm and a miraculous breeze that sprang up in the evening across the Isthmus. I wanted to follow Malinche's trail east toward Potonchan and Xicalango, even though I knew that both cities had vanished long ago. I took a bus to the steaming, raucous city of Villa Hermosa, where, at the anthropological museum, I could make some enquiries.

The desk attendant frowned. 'Palenque, you mean.'

'No, Potonchan,' I replied. 'It was down the river from here, somewhere near present-day Frontera, I believe.'

But the attendant had never heard of Potonchan. She shrugged and returned to her work, leaving me to search through the archaeological charts on the counter, until I found one that indicated its former site with a tiny triangle.

I held the paper up triumphantly for her to see, but she was unmoved. I couldn't blame her. Potonchan is not a name that anyone much remembers now. It left no soaring pyramids like the earlier Mayan cities, like glorious Chichen Itza, like Palenque or Tikal. Potonchan had been a far more mundane place, concerned principally with commerce rather than with high ritual.

Outside the museum beneath a sullen sky I watched the mighty Grijalva River plough its way past me on its slow, implacable journey toward the coast. I knew that the place where Potonchan once stood was somewhere near Frontera, where the river emptied into the Gulf of Mexico.

I walked back along the tow-path that links the museum to central Villa Hermosa, past smouldering rubbish and pungent smoke suspended in the torpid air. Students shouted to passers-by from a second-floor window. The city centre swarmed with people. I wanted to leave this place.

That evening there was trouble in Villa Hermosa. But first there was dancing in the plaza to a feverish mambo which had throbbed its way across the Caribbean Sea. It rang out through giant speakers balanced in the branches of two old silk-cotton trees, while a local official from Colosio's party prepared to address the crowd.

The party's new posters were everywhere throughout the country now, the familiar acronym PRI blazoned across the Mexican tricolour, along with one dramatic word: 'Colosio!' They had appeared, with a swiftness unheard of in Mexico, the very day following his assassination.

It didn't help the party's cause. 'They will do anything to win,' people told me. 'In sixty years they have never been out of office, but now they know they are going to lose. You will see. They'll use Colosio's death for sympathy votes.'

But I was taken by surprise when the party official rose to speak and a defiant taunt erupted from the crowd. 'Colosio!' the people chanted, 'Colosio! PRI killed Colosio!' Conspiracy theories had abounded since the moment of his death, but this one accusing his own party of his murder was an allegation I had not heard until now.

The official was unable to begin. I watched for several deafening minutes, until finally he gave up and walked away from the microphone. The chant continued, and there were mutterings of concern from the party men standing near me at the back of the crowd.

I left as the steaming rain began to fall. I took a taxi to the bus station to buy my ticket for the next morning and saw the armed guards checking the coaches leaving for Chiapas, where the Mayan uprising was continuing. I had tender memories of the places in the midst of these troubles. I had spent many tranquil months there twenty years earlier, but I felt relieved that this time my destination lay in another direction.

The road to Frontera was luxuriant with banana and cacao plantations, and there were flimsy villages and roadside stalls along the way. On the bus I heard a man and woman behind me conversing in a curious Germanic tongue. I turned to see if I could make out who they were but the bus was too crowded.

Before we reached Frontera, however, they made their way toward the front, still deep in conversation, moving carefully among the passengers standing in the aisle, and I saw immediately by their clothes that they were Mennonites. How could I possibly have forgotten the presence of these Europeans in this region?

Years before, in a town not far from here, I had seen others like them, during my first visit to Mexico. They had come rattling into town in their quaint buggies, the men in straw hats and blue overalls, the women in bonnets with virtuous pinafores covering their long, faded dresses. They had chosen to live like a tribe of ruddy giants in a world of copper-skinned Lilliputians, where they were liked and respected. How strange that these faithful Protestants had found the refuge they desired so very far from home, in Catholic Mexico. They were descendants, like the Amish, of sixteenth-century Anabaptists. Like the Amish, they had fled Europe during the seventeenth century to escape religious persecution.

I watched as they climbed awkwardly from the bus, clasping their carefully wrapped parcels in their freckled hands. The man was so huge that I was able to watch his progress along the village street for some time, until finally his straw hat disappeared around a distant corner and I lost sight of him for good.

I was heading beyond Frontera to the former site of Xicalango. The bus rattled on east along a narrow highway, with the waters of the Gulf of Mexico on one side, the Laguna de Pom on the other, a fiery salsa playing loudly on the radio. In this remote corner of Mexico, I felt closer to Havana than to Mexico City.

When I asked the driver to let me out just beyond the village of Atasta, he looked alarmed. 'I'm an archeologist, *señor*,' I lied, but it was explanation enough. He told me the next bus back to Frontera would come through in another two hours. It would be just enough time for my purposes.

There is nothing in this remote eastern corner of Mexico to mark the site of Xicalango. Nothing to suggest that in the days before the arrival of the Spanish, merchants from throughout Meso America travelled here to the lagoon's shores. They came to exchange jaguar and ocelot skins, gold and copper ornaments, copal incense, topaz, jade and turquoise lip plugs, chocolate, precious quetzal feathers, and slaves, like Malinche.

The merchants spoke a multitude of languages and in normal circumstances would have been divided by innumerable political and cultural enmities, but at Xicalango they mingled freely beneath the expedient mantle of commerce. Xicalango was a Samarkand of the Americas. The Conquest, of course, changed this forever. Those great mercantile pilgrimages came to an end, although the town of Xicalango lingered for a time. Then the epidemics began and soon only wild cattle were left to graze among the empty stone warehouses and broken-down jetties.

During the early years of the seventeenth century, Xicalango was inhabited once more, when it became a temporary haven for French and English pirates from across the Caribbean, and later a camp for English loggers from Jamaica with their African slaves. They called Xicalango 'Beef Island' and the Palizada River 'Logwood Creek'. Such bleak, pragmatic names for such a beautiful place. At some point a ship is said to have arrived from New England with twenty Iroquois or Delaware captives aboard who escaped into the hinterland and settled down with Mayan women. By the end of the eighteenth century Xicalango was silent and deserted once more.

I spread my map on the ground and found the Palizada River. I traced its thin blue journey with my finger, from the point where it branches off from the larger Usumacinta River meandering in from Guatemala. That's the way the merchants must have brought Malinche, I thought. They must have slipped quietly along the stream in their canoes, following this same filigree of streams and coastal estuaries I was now tracing on the map, until they made their way here, to Xicalango.

From Jaltipan to this sheltered place was a journey of some 250 kilometres. For me it had only amounted to a few hours travel. In sixteenth-century Mexico it was a voyage to another world. From the roadside I watched the waterbirds stalking in the rushes, as a shrimp fisherman dragged his net gently through the quiet waters of the lagoon.

Back at Frontera I looked out across the Grijalva River to the empty mangroves where Potonchan once stood. As with Xicalango, there is nothing left to see. Not even the name has survived.

Potonchan was also once a wealthy trading centre, but aligned exclusively with the Mayan world and more limited in scope, therefore, than its cosmopolitan neighbour on the Laguna de Pom. It too survived for a time after the Conquest, with a new name, Santa Maria de la Victoria, until one devastating plague after another was unleashed on its unfortunate people. 'A

prelude

pestilence seized them,' a Franciscan monk recalled later, 'characterised by great pustules, which rotted their bodies with a great stench.'

When pirates arrived to finish off what the epidemics had begun, the city was abandoned. But not quite forever. Several more attempts at resettlement were made but each one failed, and the little churches and houses so optimistically constructed fell into ruins. It is significant that the last of these settlements was called Dolores, a name so suggestive of the suffering this place has known.

Malinche's last year in Potonchan was 1518. It was also the end of the strange twenty-seven-year pause between Columbus's arrival in the Caribbean islands in 1492 and Cortés's invasion of the mainland in 1519. The Mayans among whom Malinche was living must have been aware of the unfamiliar presence in the islands to their east just 200 kilometres across the Caribbean. In 1502 a Mayan trading party had come upon Columbus himself as he made his way around the Gulf of Honduras. Nine years later, in 1511, a handful of Spanish castaways, survivors of a shipwreck near Jamaica, had been washed up on Mayan shores.

But in spite of these early encounters and that flurry of foreign activity in the islands, life on the mainland went on, as far as we can tell, more or less as it had done for millennia. The word 'America', so familiar to us now, had yet to be invented. If the diverse peoples of this complex ancient world, Malinche's world, possessed a collective name for themselves, it would soon be obliterated forever by Columbus's famous misnomer, 'Indian'.

In 1518 a contemporary of Cortés crossed from Cuba with a

small fleet to explore the mainland coast, which was still largely uncharted. His name was Juan de Grijalva. Grijalva entered the series of tranquil lagoons where Xicalango lay hidden. He repaired his ships and explored a little, but he did not see the port of trade spread out along the banks of the more secluded Laguna de Pom.

When he sailed on further down the coast, however, he did see Potonchan. His chaplain, a man called Juan Diaz, left an account of their experiences there, and his narrative provides the only glimpse we have of Potonchan before its rapid and painful decline began.

It was 8 June 1518 when Grijalva's fleet reached the mouth of the immense river that still bears his name. Fresh water had been a problem throughout their voyage, and they recorded with joy that the river poured with such might into the ocean that 'we drew up drinking water almost six miles at sea'. From their ships they could just make out a fine city. They saw a timber palisade along the riverbank and beyond this the town itself, handsome and well laid out with many grand houses. The principal square was flanked by pyramid temples and at its centre stood a huge and ancient silk-cotton tree.

Grijalva's chaplain, Juan Diaz, was mightily impressed by Potonchan's people too. 'The inhabitants are striking in appearance,' he said, 'tall and fit for battle. They have bows, swords and round shields.' The elegant residents of Potonchan were, in fact, the Chontal Maya, members of that great civilisation of astronomers and mathematicians that had ruled Central America since time immemorial. But the chaplain called them simply 'Indians'. 'The men of this province,' he noted with enthusiasm, 'excelled in beauty and stature all the other Indians.'

The Spaniards anchored in the mouth of the river and waited, and the people of Potonchan waited too, and after three days of mutual observation the Mayan ruler came out to greet the foreign fleet in a large canoe escorted by a great flotilla of warriors. He boarded Grijalva's flagship and presented the captain with a treasury of splendid gifts: wooden masks inlaid with turquoise, strings of hollow gold beads, necklaces of beaten gold, ornate featherwork, tiny golden ducks and lizards.

Grijalva responded with a mirror, green glass beads, scissors and a pair of knives. It is a depressingly familiar catalogue, and some years later one of the first historians of the Indies would slyly remark that 'all this among the Christians was of very little value as can be well understood'.

Apparently undaunted, the lord of Potonchan began to adorn Grijalva in a suit of wooden armour overlaid with gold leaf, piece by piece, 'and on his head he put a gold crown, only the crown was made of very thin gold leaf'. Grijalva improvised his own response to this elegant ritual. He presented his regal visitor with a green velvet doublet, red stockings, a sash, a velvet cap and some black leather sandals.

The Mayan put them on and for some time the two men stood together beneath the gaze of their attendants, each confronted with a mirror image of himself superimposed onto an alien face and figure. The chaplain, Juan Diaz, recalled later that Grijalva's beauty, as he stood there glinting in the sun, was incomparable.

There is one more fragment to this Potonchan story. Grijalva was made to understand that it was also customary for the leaders to exchange names. This was done and the warriors of Potonchan returned to their shores crying Grijalva's name out loud, like a trophy of war, but we are never told what name the lord of Potonchan gave Grijalva in return. At least one Mayan scholar has suggested that it may have been Acipac, hispanicised after the Conquest into the surname Azbaque, and reflected now in the name of the state: Tabasco. In any case, this Mayan lord who may have been called Acipac returned to Potonchan, but before he went he advised the Spaniards that if gold was what they sought they should sail on west.

That other Diaz, the soldier–chronicler Bernal Diaz, who would later accompany Cortés, was also present on this earlier voyage to the mainland. In his memoirs he recalled that the Mayan kept repeating 'Colua, Colua', 'Mexico, Mexico', and pointing west in the direction of the setting sun. 'But we did not know,' Bernal Diaz said, 'what nature of thing *Colua* was, nor *Mexico*.' These words were the name of a people, but he had no way of knowing that yet.

There is no record of Malinche or of any other woman present at this historic meeting between Mayan and Spaniard. She must certainly have heard talk, however, of the strange fleet anchored in the mouth of the river during this, her last year in Potonchan, and may well have glimpsed it from behind the town's palisade.

Grijalva did sail west and his progress was observed by the mysterious 'Colua-Mexica' who watched the fleet's progress along the coast and carried news of the strangers back to their great city in the mountains. Their words were reported later in the Florentine Codex, precious words because they offer the first documented description of Europeans by indigenous Americans.

'They were very white,' the observers told their emperor. 'Their eyes were like chalk. Their hair — on some it was yellow, on some it was black. They wore long beards; they were yellow too. And there were some black-skinned ones with kinky hair.' This last was a reference to the African and mulatto slaves who had accompanied the expedition.

As for the Spaniards, they were enthralled by all they saw and urged Grijalva to conquer and settle. But his orders had been strictly to explore the coastline and return, so despite their entreaties he sailed his fleet back to Cuba, where his uncle, the governor, and all the other New World adventurers waiting there, received joyful news of his voyage.

Grijalva's chaplain is long forgotten now. He was just another of those small players who slip so easily from the pages of history, but his journal is important because it was the first eyewitness account of mainland America to be published in Europe. It first appeared in Italy in 1519 and was used as a source by the early historians of the Indies such as Peter Martyr and Gonzalo Fernandez de Oviedo. So for a brief time, until it was superseded by news of Cortés's great conquest, the narrative of Juan Diaz enjoyed a certain celebrity in learned European circles.

The chaplain was impressed by what he saw at Potonchan, but profoundly disappointed by Grijalva's behaviour. He complained, for example, that when the fleet was attacked by 'indians' as it skirted the coast, 'the captain forbade us . . . when we wished to pursue them and lay waste their town with fire and sword'. He said that he and the crew urged Grijalva to plunder the rich and fertile lands they saw, but in vain. 'If we had had a proper captain,' moans this worldly priest, 'we would have taken from this country in only one month about three hundred thousand *castellanos*.'

Juan de Grijalva seems to have been a moderate and law-abiding man, qualities that did him little good in such a maverick age. Soon after his return to Cuba he was sent to the colony of Tierra Firme, now known as Panama, and from there to Nicaragua, where he died in some forgotten battle.

But things went better for his disgruntled chaplain, for a while at least. Just a few months later this ambitious cleric set sail once more, with a 'proper captain' this time. He returned to Potonchan with his hopes rekindled, and he was there when Malinche made her entrance into the historic record.

It happened the following year, in March 1519. Hernan Cortés's fleet arrived in Potonchan, but after Grijalva's visit the city had been desolated by a new and unknown disease, probably its first taste of smallpox, and its people wanted no more of these death-bearing foreigners.

This time there were no elaborate robing ceremonies, no rituals of gift or name exchange, just an unambiguous display of hostility from a legion of warriors amassed along the shores to the east of the town. A fierce battle took place, the first great battle on the American mainland between European soldiers and

Amerindian warriors. The Maya were formidable as always, but in this, their first encounter with the explosive weaponry of Europe, they suffered a crushing defeat.

Bernal Diaz del Castillo was there that day in Potonchan, for he had signed on with Cortés in Cuba. Many years later Diaz recalled the propitiary gifts the Mayan nobles of Potonchan brought forward in surrender. 'Four diadems,' he said, 'some ornaments in the form of lizards, two shaped like little dogs and five little ducks, also some earrings, some masks of indian faces, two gold soles for sandals.'

But all this was nothing, he said, compared with the twenty women presented to them. Bernal Diaz could not remember all their names, 'and there is no reason for naming any of them', he said, except to record that they were the first women baptised as Christians on the American mainland. But there was one he did recall: 'A very excellent person who was called doña Marina, this being her name after she was baptised.'

Marina. A Christian echo of Malinalli, or possibly its Mayan equivalent, Malina? Whatever the transliterative possibilities, this woman, it seems, was the child from Jaltipan. Diaz said she was a woman of fine appearance and confident bearing, and whenever he spoke of her in his memoirs, he used that reverential title, *doña*. He said she was a woman of great presence, or literally, of great being: '*La doña Marina tenia mucho ser.*'

Bernal Diaz said it was 15 March 1519 when Malinche was handed over to the Spaniards. It is one of very few certainties in her story. She may have been a woman of some presence but she must still have been young, perhaps little more than eighteen or nineteen years of age. It is also possible she had a child with her.

In later years, during an inquest held into Cortés's conduct after the Conquest, several old conquistadors would recall a child called Catalina, whom they had taken to be Malinche's daughter, or her niece, a young girl who survived the Conquest and lived with Malinche for a time in Cortés's household. Like so much about Malinche this rumour is vague and unverifiable, yet persistent enough to suggest that there may be some truth in it. We know even less about the other women who went with her to the Spaniards, but it is probable that like her they were foreign slaves or concubines, drawn from the most vulnerable margins of Potonchan society.

An old, romanticised engraving of this moment is held in The Bancroft Library at the University of California in Berkeley. Malinche, or Marina as she was now called, stands coyly on the banks of the Grijalva, at the forefront of a cluster of women. Like the others she is naked but her long and lustrous hair curls modestly about her body, like the Botticelli Venus. Behind her in the river is a sailing ship, before her stands Cortés. In contrast to her, he is fully clothed in elegant European attire, and he greets her in courtly fashion.

This pleasant, idyllic portrait is a relic of the days when it was still possible to ignore the truth about what happens to women in war and conquest. It is an absurd fiction and it tells us nothing about the undoubted terror of Malinche's predicament.

The incident at Potonchan was the first of many occasions on which indigenous leaders handed over women servants,

MALINCHE IS PRESENTED TO CORTÉS
AT POTONCHAN, MARCH, 1519
(engraving from The Bancroft Library,
University of California)

concubines, daughters and nieces, to the Spaniards. Bernal Diaz spoke openly about this custom and it often passes without comment, perhaps because it became so commonplace during the Conquest. Or perhaps because of history's implicit understanding that women are the spoils of war. It was not until Bosnia that rape was at last defined as a war crime.

The giving of women to the enemy was a venerable Amerindian custom that the Spaniards would encounter again and again with relish during the years that followed. The Mayan lords of Potonchan intended their gift as a peace offering. If all went according to plan, it would provide them with some breathing space, even a possible alliance with these invaders. To the victorious Spaniards the captive women were an invaluable part of their booty. Bernal Diaz makes this clear in his own comment that 'all this was nothing compared to the twenty women' they were given. To him and to his comrades the Mayan gift of women meant servants to prepare their food, to carry water and collect firewood, to tend their wounds, and to provide sexual services.

As for the women themselves, we know nothing of their feelings on the matter, for who knows anything about the lives of slaves? We can guess, however, that what this tradition meant to them was fear and forcible separation from everything and everyone they knew, the shock of foreign men with strange, hirsute, malodorous bodies and unknown sexual habits, and a life of unimaginable toil for an alien army on the move.

Malinche and the women who went with her to the Spaniards were not warriors. They had not been trained since childhood to display fearless courage in the face of battle. But the ordeal the city fathers of Potonchan forced them to endure was another kind of war, requiring a different kind of bravery, as they went forward to meet whatever awaited them at the hands of the enemy.

The fortunate would be attached to one man, the less fortunate became the property of many. Malinche may have been among the more favoured of the women, for Bernal Diaz tells us that in Potonchan that day Cortés gave her to his close friend Hernando Alonso Puertocarrero, 'a very grand gentleman and a cousin of the Count of Medellin'. We do not know what happened to the other women. Neither their names nor their eventual fate were ever recorded.

A few days later, on Palm Sunday 1519, the fleet set sail for its journey down the coast toward the land of the 'Colua-Mexica', which had so enticed Grijalva's men the previous year, and Malinche went with them with her new name, and her new god, and perhaps with a child in tow.

⚜

It was nearly May and I was still shambling along the gulf coast. I had breathed the languid, salty air, and seen the empty mangroves where Potonchan once stood. I had seen the lagoon banks of former Xicalango. I had followed Malinche's fragile trail this far and I needed to rest, to leave her story for a while. I boarded an early morning bus from Frontera and took the road east once more. We passed the site of Xicalango but this time I stayed on the bus, which was bound for the bitter dry limestone of the Yucatan Peninsula.

Mexico beyond Frontera remains the realm of the Maya. Not just in the shadows of the great abandoned pyramids of Uxmal and Chichen Itza, but in the quiet villages with their pigs and hens and ragged children, and their Mayan names which have never been hispanicised, lavish, ancient names such as Xascabcheb and Uxkakaltok.

I was barely awake when we reached the little town of Chenkan and crossed a stream flowing into the Gulf of Mexico. In the half-light of dawn I saw that the Mayan woman on the other side of the aisle from me was awake. I leaned across and asked her if she spoke Spanish. She said she did. I asked her if she knew what this river was called, and she answered me quietly, speaking in a whisper so as not to wake the other passengers. 'Malinche,' she said. 'It's called Malinche.'

I watched this silent memorial to Malinche recede into the distance, here in this obscure place, not far from Xicalango and Potonchan, and thought how in Mexico she has been excluded from the ostentatious world of marble and alabaster statues, but she inhabits the more secluded realm of streams and hidden gardens instead. Official memory is powerful but it has its limitations.

Gift of Tongues

I made my way back west after that, to the glistening coastal city of Veracruz. Its warmth lifted my spirits after the sullen heat of the south. Bright and clear, with ships riding at anchor, modern container vessels now, where galleons and caravels had once sheltered in its safe harbour.

My friend in Mexico City, Filomena Alvarado, had told me that when I reached Veracruz I must find my way to the plaza. It was the most beautiful plaza, she said, in all of Mexico. A large stringed orchestra of elderly musicians was playing beneath the palm trees the evening I arrived, and I rang her from a telephone box to tell her she was right. 'There's something here for you,' she told me. It was a package from the Archivo General de Indias in Seville, documents I had ordered some weeks earlier. I asked her to keep them safe for me until I returned.

Next day I sat alone in Parque Zamora, eating fish a woman had fried for me in the market. I had bought a small cold bottle of beer from her too, and I drank it greedily. I walked to the harbour and along the wharves toward the island Juan de Grijalva's men had called 'San Juan de Ulua' in an extravagant tangle of references. 'San Juan' for St John and for Grijalva himself. 'Ulua' for the elusive Culua-Mexica, in whose political domain the island lay.

Nowadays we know the Culua-Mexica better as the Aztecs. Sometime in the twelfth century they had wandered into the central valley of Mexico from some distant place in the north called Aztlan. It is a Nahuatl word, *Aztlan*, meaning the place of the white feathered heron.

The entry of these nomads into the valley was not welcomed. Those who watched their arrival were urbane and civilised peoples who had lived around the shores of Lake Texcoco for centuries. They reviled the newcomers as barbarians and called them *Azteca*, 'the people of heron place'. The name was intended as an insult, a reminder of their humble origins in the north, of their parvenu status in the rich and fertile valley.

But within a hundred years of their arrival in the valley, the people of heron place had silenced their detractors. They had laid waste their cities, captured their gods and constructed their own great metropolis, Tenochtitlan, on whose ruins Mexico City now stands. Along the way they had discarded their humble title 'Aztec' and acquired a more dignified name, 'Culua-Mexica', to symbolise their newly elevated status as conquerors of the valley.

When I first read Bernal Diaz I was puzzled by these words 'Culua-Mexica' or 'Colua', as he usually spelled it. He always called the Aztecs by this name, as did Cortés in his despatches to the King of Spain, and the Mayan lord of Potonchan when he sent the Spaniards on their way west. 'Aztec' is not a word you will find anywhere in contemporary sixteenth-century accounts of the Spanish Conquest. It is a curiosity, a throwback, as incongruous a designation for the sixteenth-century Culua-Mexica as the term 'Viking' would be for a modern-day Icelander.

History is full of such linguistic accidents: misspellings, mispronunciations, misunderstandings replicated over hundreds of years, like computer viruses. In this case, the great twentieth-century scholar Robert Barlow blamed the great eighteenth-century scholar Francisco Javier Clavijero for the loss of Culua-Mexica.

Barlow said the archaic and obsolete term 'Aztec' first appeared in Clavijero's work. Where Clavijero got it from is uncertain, but Barlow claimed that after that it was copied faithfully and mistakenly by subsequent historians. Modern scholars detest it for its inaccuracy, but this word, with its two strident syllables and its potent connotations, is too well entrenched in the popular imagination to be relinquished now.

This is lamentable in many ways, not the least because Culua-Mexica, pronounced *cool-wah mesheeka,* is such a beautiful and sonorous name. But it is not just the sound that is lost. It is the story the name encapsulates, the narrative of a peoples' journey out of the wilderness, of their short-lived but glorious passage through human history. All that remains now of that plangent, evocative name, is the fragile echo we hear whispering through that more familiar word, 'Mexico'.

When Malinche came to what is now Veracruz, in April 1519, the present city did not exist. There were only empty sand dunes and mosquitoes. The expedition in which she found herself was not an official army regiment. It was an industrious multilingual commercial enterprise on the move, with every essential trade and profession represented: soldiers, blacksmiths, merchants, carpenters, surgeons, tailors, notaries, such as Cortés himself, and the odd idle aristocrat, including Puertocarrero, to whom Malinche had been given at Potonchan.

There were several hundred Spaniards, a handful of Portuguese and some Italians, together with an unknown number of African slaves, and 'indian' captives from across the Caribbean, survivors of Colombus's invasion twenty-seven years earlier. There was also a small and surprising cluster of Spanish women, whose names, by some miracle, have survived in the records: Francisca and Beatriz de Ordaz, Elvira and Beatriz Hernandez, Caterina Marquez, Isabel Rodriguez and Maria de Vera. They were the sisters, the wives and daughters, of the men in Cortés's expedition.

Through the camp moved an oddity with the cropped hair of a Mayan, although he was not a Mayan but a Spaniard and a priest. His name was Geronimo de Aguilar. His life so far had been almost as strange as Malinche's, and at Veracruz their paths converged for a time.

Aguilar had been a passenger on a Spanish ship that went down on some rocks near Jamaica in 1511. He had struggled ashore somewhere on the coast near Mexico's present border with Belize, and had managed to survive there for the next eight years, among the people he called the Maia. Like Malinche, who was by then living not far around the coast at Potonchan, Aguilar learned to speak the Mayan language, but he never reconciled himself to his situation. He prayed each day for deliverance, and his prayers were answered when Cortés crossed the Caribbean to the mainland coast.

Bernal Diaz was present when Aguilar stumbled before them. He said they mistook him for a Mayan at first, with his cropped hair, his ragged loincloth and his skin darkened by exposure to the sun. Until suddenly Aguilar cried out in halting Spanish, 'Are you Christians? God and Saint Mary of Seville!' Then to their amazement he fell to his knees and asked if it was Wednesday. Throughout his eight years among the Maya, Aguilar had kept faithful count of the days, with the breviary he carried by his side in an old net bag.

Diaz recalled that Cortés wrapped Aguilar in a cloak and offered him food and drink. When he had calmed his unfortunate compatriot Cortés began to question him closely about this land in which he had spent those wretched years. Aguilar replied that as a person of lowly rank among the Maya he had learned very little. 'Only . . . about hewing wood,' he said, 'and drawing water.' But at least he spoke the Mayan tongue and he told the Spaniards he would be 'a useful and faithful interpreter' for them.

He brought disturbing news, however, about another Spaniard, a fellow castaway who had survived the shipwreck with him. This man, whose name was Gonzalo Guerrero, had tattooed his face and married a Mayan woman, Aguilar told them. Guerrero had raised children with her and had become a leading warrior. He had even directed an attack on a Spanish fleet which had touched the coastline a few years earlier. Aguilar said he had implored Guerrero to leave with him, to join Cortés while they had the opportunity, but Guerrero had refused.

The Spaniards never forgot about Guerrero. His inexplicable presence out there among the Maya seemed to haunt them, and from time to time in the years that followed they made attempts to persuade him back to the Spanish fold. But he remained faithful to the Maya, even when the tide of conquest turned hopelessly against them.

Guerrero's strange story is in many ways a mirror image of Malinche's. He entered her world, while she entered his. It was an unintended, involuntary exchange at first, but in the end both appear to have embraced their adoptive people.

In 1535, in the aftermath of a great battle, the Spaniards found Guerrero's body washed up on a shore in Honduras. The dead man bore all the insignia of a Mayan warrior, but he was unquestionably a European. Guerrero died doing battle against his former countrymen, and, like Malinche, he went to his grave an enigma.

⚜

The French historian, Jacques Soustelle, once described pre-Conquest Mexico as a mosaic of cities, and I have always admired his elegant metaphor: a mosaic composed of different cultures, separate languages, distinct histories. The linguistic fragmentation of this complex world, this rich mosaic, is the essence of Malinche's story.

The Culua-Mexica were Nahuatl speakers, but as Bernal Diaz associated this language exclusively with them, he called it by their name: *Culua*, or *Colua*. 'This language is here common to the allies of Mexico and Moctezuma,' he wrote, 'just as Latin was formerly common to those of Rome.' Although the Spaniards hadn't realised at the time, when they sailed west from Potonchan they had left the Mayan realm and its vernacular far behind. When they entered the political domain of the Culua-Mexica they found that their interpreter, Geronimo de Aguilar, knew nothing of the Culua language and he was silenced once more.

The situation posed an urgent challenge for Cortés. Intelligence gathering and artful communication were his preferred weapons, and like Juan de Grijalva before him he had taken Mayan captives from time to time as he sailed around the Caribbean coast, in the hope of training them as interpreters. None of these experiments had worked. That is why the discovery of Aguilar had been so important to Cortés. But suddenly Aguilar too was unable to assist.

There is a story, perhaps apocryphal, that in the midst of the Spaniards' concern someone overheard Malinche conversing in Nahuatl with some local women who were grinding corn. It may have been Aguilar himself. His ear would have been well enough attuned to Mayan to know a different native language when he heard it. He may well have been searching for a Nahuatl–Mayan speaker to help shore up his own position in the expedition. Or perhaps it was one of the Spanish women, observing the grinding of corn by the Mayan captives, who distinguished the different sounds of this new language and realised the strategic importance of what she had heard.

Bernal Diaz tells it this way. He says that when the first of

Moctezuma's emissaries arrived Aguilar was clearly flummoxed and could make nothing of what they said. Nor could he make himself understood by them. But Malinche, who was present at the time, seemed to understand what they were saying, and in response to their incomprehensible enquiries, she pointed toward Cortés.

It was a defining moment in her story. The visitors turned and bowed and 'paid him great marks of respect in their fashion'. According to Diaz the revelation of her language skills was as incidental and as providential as that. She simply saw her chance and grasped it.

However it occurred, it seems that sometime around Easter 1519 the Spaniards discovered that this woman they called Marina spoke both Mayan and Nahuatl, and since Aguilar spoke Mayan and Spanish, she might just provide the urgent communications link they required for their dealings with the Culua-Mexica.

This then was how Malinche came to the attention of Cortés, because the ability to talk, to persuade, to reason, to enquire, to 'discover the secrets' of these new lands was always an essential strategy to him. Her needs, however, were far more urgent and fundamental than his.

She was a young woman without country or family. She had been passed from hand to hand, from her parents to the men from Xicalango, from them to some anonymous Mayan lord in Potonchan, and finally to the Spaniards. Bilinguilism is frequently the bitter fruit of exile, and so it was in Malinche's case. Her bilingual voice was emblematic of her misfortunes, but suddenly it offered her the protection, however temporary, of the commander of this strange expedition.

It was April 1519, the year One Reed by the Aztec calendar, and Bernal Diaz said later that it was at this moment that their Conquest truly began. 'I have made a point of explaining this matter,' he continued, 'because without the help of doña Marina we could not have understood the language of New Spain and Mexico.'

From that day on, a curious chain was forged, linking Cortés to Aguilar to Malinche to Moctezuma's emissaries, as they came and went on their visits to the invaders' camp. Diplomatic niceties were attended to, intelligence was gathered, information was exchanged, backwards and forwards in Nahuatl, Mayan, Spanish.

It was absurd, unwieldy, a translator's nightmare, an epistemological maze which we can only wonder at as we recall that each time Cortés said this, or Moctezuma said that, their words were conveyed through this trilingual chain of voices. And that, in spite of 'the reassuring inverted commas', as the historian Inga Clendinnen calls them, with which Cortés's grandiloquent speeches are reported, we have no way of knowing how accurately his words were conveyed by Malinche to Moctezuma's emissaries. Nor did Cortés himself. But whatever the imperfections of this extraordinary system, he had no option but to trust this young woman with his precious words, for she alone offered a path along which he could begin to make his way.

'In every human utterance lies the sum total of that person's linguistic past.' So says Andreas Fine Licht in Peter Hoeg's novel

Miss Smilla's Feeling for Snow. Fine Licht then proceeds to trace Smilla's life through her accent, as she listens in amazement at his accuracy.

'Grew up in Thule or north of it. One or both parents Inuit. Came to Denmark after assimilating the entire linguistic foundation of Greenlandic . . . a trace of North Sealand accent. And strangely enough, a hint of West Greenlandic.'

If we could hear Malinche speak, if we were educated sixteenth-century Nahuatl speakers, what would we detect in her speech? The remnants of an Isthmus dialect, a trace of Chontal Mayan, even a hint of the despised Popoluca?

We cannot be sure where Malinche learned Nahuatl, but we know she acquired it either as a first or second language somewhere in those southern lands where she had spent her life so far. Her pronunciation must have rung with provincial inflections which only Moctezuma's ambassadors, of all the people listening to her, could have recognised.

These noblemen had arrived on the coast, and through the improbable new interpreting team of Aguilar and Malinche they had made their formal greetings of welcome. They presented Cortés with turquoise masks, a giant disc of gold and one of silver, a shield decorated with shimmering quetzal feathers.

No one tells us how the emissaries responded to Malinche. Did they recognise, in her dress, in her accent, in her demeanour, certain signs that Bernal Diaz, as an outsider, could not see? The accoutrements of a concubine, the vulgarity of a barbarian? Perhaps, as Inga Clendinnen suggests in her luminous study *Aztecs*, Malinche's very vocal presence beside Cortés dismayed and disconcerted the ambassadors to an extent that we would find difficult to comprehend.

Clendinnen describes the sacred exclusivity of public speech among the Culua-Mexica. Taking as her authority the Florentine Codex, that encyclopaedia of Culua-Mexica culture compiled by young Nahuatl scholars after the Conquest, she concludes that women in Culua-Mexica society had no right to speak 'on high public occasions', nor to sing, nor play music, in public. Women's tongues, she believes, were strictly curbed in the realm of public life, of state affairs. So the sound of Malinche's voice as she participated in these high diplomatic discussions probably shocked Moctezuma's ambassadors to the bone.

Malinche would have known, must have known, that she was breaking a great taboo when she did what she did at Veracruz. It would have taken extraordinary courage to speak in the presence of the noblemen from Tenochtitlan, but courage is a quality she must have possessed in abundance. How else could she have survived her turbulent life to this point?

Toughness has rarely been considered appealing in a woman. We like our heroines dead or dying, tragic and vulnerable. But here is Malinche: young, strong, clever, determined to survive, perhaps with a child to protect. She knows she must attach herself to the leader, somehow. She must offer him something more precious than mere sexuality, which is a commodity available from any of the other women. Language! She can offer him language, explanation, interpretation. With her gift of tongues she will draw aside the curtain on the new world he seeks.

So, after Easter 1519, Malinche becomes famous for her voice. She deciphers and communicates to all those who listen, the glory and terror of Cortés's elaborate discourse as their expedition makes its slow, momentous way up through the mountains toward the Culua-Mexica capital, Tenochtitlan.

For the next two years it is possible to follow Malinche's footsteps with some certainty. We know where she went, the approximate dates and with whom. She is there behind the public face, the public voice, just visible on the horizon, a solitary female figure. Her words are conveyed to us by Bernal Diaz, but the inner woman remains hidden from us, always.

II

conquest

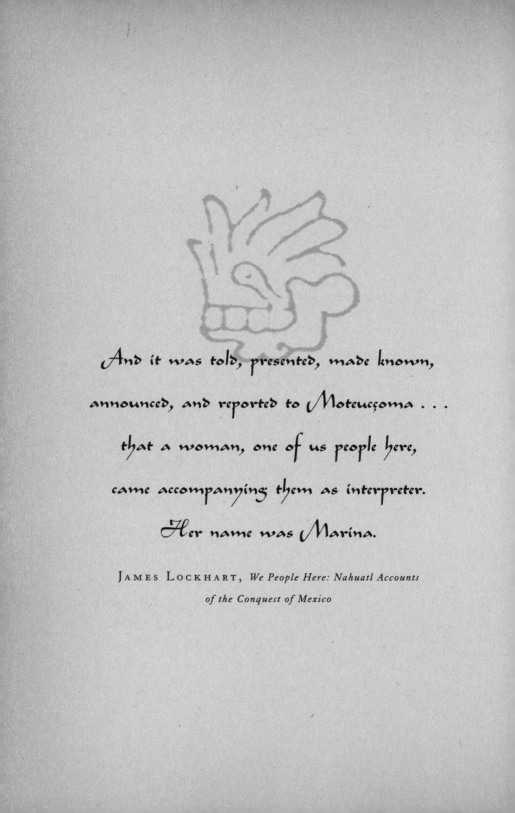

And it was told, presented, made known,

announced, and reported to Moteucçoma . . .

that a woman, one of us people here,

came accompanying them as interpreter.

Her name was Marina.

JAMES LOCKHART, *We People Here: Nahuatl Accounts of the Conquest of Mexico*

Malinche

It was June now, and on the coast the rains were beginning. The beautiful city of Veracruz was damp and forlorn, like a resort closing down for the winter, except that in tropical latitudes like this, it is the summer which drives away the musicians and the balloon sellers and the tourists. I too was anxious to leave, to return to the capital. I longed for company and conversation, for the anonymity of the metropolis. The birds chattered and rustled in the dripping trees above me as I walked through the plaza for the last time.

The road to what was once Tenochtitlan is the road to Mexico City now. It is a hundred times more direct than the tortuous paths Malinche followed with Cortés and Bernal Diaz in August 1519, up and down through the ribbon of towering volcanoes which lie between the coast and the capital.

The country through which they travelled was nominally part of the Culua-Mexica tributary empire, but its traditional owners were the Totonac. The Totonac spoke Nahuatl because it was essential for their dealings with their Culua-Mexica overlords, but they preferred their own language, their own customs. They welcomed the Spaniards as potential allies. They were unwilling subjects of Moctezuma, and they had never given up hope of reclaiming their independence.

Bernal Diaz writes that in the beautiful Totonac city of Jalapa, the Spaniards proclaimed the truths of their holy religion 'through doña Marina and Geronimo de Aguilar'. So Malinche was a preacher now, the first Nahuatl-speaking evangelist in the Americas. In our cynical age it is easy to assume that she was mouthing the words she heard in Mayan from Aguilar's lips, but perhaps she was a sincere convert. The men and women of this strange multiracial company were probably as much her people now as any of the other strangers she had learned to live among since she was taken from her home in the Isthmus.

I was reading *The Vortex*, by the Colombian novelist, Jose Eustacio Rivera. Filomena had given it to me in Mexico City. One of the characters was a half-caste woman, a *mulatta*, who made me think, in her composure, her solitude and statelessness, of Malinche. 'Where is your country?' the *mulatta* is asked. 'Here, where I am,' she replies. 'And where is your God?' 'There, where the sun comes up.'

Bernal Diaz was a meticulous writer but not a stylist like the academicians of his time. In his memoirs he apologises frequently for his lack of stylish prose, but for us his plain words and his childlike ingenuousness are his great strengths. The comparisons he draws, as he seeks to describe the strange and exotic world of the Americas, are intriguing. Such and such a thing was just like what happened in the *Tales of Amadis* or in the *Ballad of Montesinos*, he says, referring to his favourite tales of chivalry. So we know what books he read. He was a devotee, apparently, of the same popular fifteenth-century fables that would one day inspire Cervantes to create his tragic Don Quixote.

Diaz's comparisons were a kind of translation, a way of drawing the strange and wonderful things he saw into his field of comprehension. His repetitions might have been tedious, especially for his later translators and editors, but his attention to detail has proved a gift to posterity. Where Malinche is concerned he is a constant witness to her presence and her role in the expedition.

Cortés announced this, Diaz says, 'through doña Marina', or ordered that, 'through doña Marina'. He has left us hundreds of such small and fleeting reminders, and if you scour his texts it is possible to find other, slightly more suggestive glimpses of her throughout those months; subtle, imperfect fragments, but precious because they are almost all we have of her.

He tells the following story, for example. As they drew close to a certain town, one of their scouts who had been sent ahead came galloping back wildly, shouting for all to hear that he had seen its walls and they were made of silver. Malinche cautioned them, warning that what the scout had probably seen was just the morning sun shining on the town's burnished, lime-coated walls. When they reached the town they saw that she was right, and Bernal Diaz says the scout was teased for ever after about this incident.

Does this tell us something about Malinche — that she was not as easily deluded as the Spanish adventurers with whom she travelled? They may have been raised on their fanciful novels of chivalry but she had been fending for herself since childhood. Hers could not have been an existence to inspire dreams.

At the Totonac town of Quiahuitzlan there was another incident. The usual felicitations were underway when suddenly a cavalcade of princely strangers arrived dressed in elaborate clothes, with their shining hair pulled back in high ponytails. Diaz said they passed the Spaniards by 'with cocksure pride'.

The villagers turned pale and prostrated themselves before the elegant visitors, offering them beautiful flowers and great quantities of chocolate, 'which is the best of their drinks'. But the strangers harangued the townspeople in Nahuatl, while Cortés and his men looked on, intrigued. Turning to Malinche, they asked who these men could be.

She had no more experience than they had with the affairs of the empire, but Diaz said she appeared to have grasped the situation perfectly and did not hesitate. The strangers, she replied calmly, were Moctezuma's tribute collectors, and they were furious with the villagers for receiving the Spaniards so warmly.

She must have been listening throughout this dialogue, with the instincts of one whose survival had depended for many years on her ability to understand, as quickly as possible, what was going on around her.

Bernal Diaz writes candidly and often in his memoirs about the fears that plagued him during that journey. As a professional soldier, anxiety and apprehension were occupational hazards, and he was never ashamed to admit to them. At the hillside town of Zautla, for example, he saw something that gave him pause. It was an enormous rack with human skulls arranged neatly in perfect, meticulous rows. To his horror he was able to count them 'and I reckoned them at more than a hundred thousand' he said. In another corner of the square he saw pyramids 'made up of innumerable thigh bones'. It was his first sight of the forlorn relics of ritual killing. The closer he came to Tenochtitlan the more such skull racks he saw.

Later, as an old man, he admitted that his greatest fear throughout the Conquest had been death by ritual sacrifice. During the battle for Tenochtitlan, he saw sixty-two fellow soldiers dragged off alive to the altar to have their chests struck open 'and their palpitating hearts cut out'. The memory of their terrible deaths made him fear death more intensely than ever before, so that when he went into battle a fit of horror and gloom would seize him 'and I would make water once or twice and commend myself to God and his blessed mother'.

The sense of his own terror seems to have made him profoundly aware of Malinche's courage. 'Let me say,' he wrote, 'that doña Marina, although a native woman, possessed such manly valour that though she heard every day that the Indians were going to kill us and eat our flesh with chillis, and though she had seen us surrounded in recent battles and knew that we were all wounded and sick, yet she betrayed no weakness but a courage greater than that of a woman.'

It is during this journey that her name 'Malinche' evolves. Bernal Diaz always referred to her as 'Marina', but he noticed that the people among whom they passed in the city states along the way called her by another name. It sounded to him like 'Malinche', but what he probably heard was 'Malintzin'. In the Nahuatl histories that appeared in the aftermath of conquest, she is usually referred to by this name.

That final syllable, *-tzin*, is a Nahuatl honorific. Like *-san* in Japanese or *doña* in Spanish, *-tzin* may be attached to a personal name to denote respect. In Diaz's mangled approximation, however, since that '-tzin' sound was so alien to his Spanish ears, the name he heard and recorded was 'Malinche'. As for 'Malin', Nahuatl has no 'r' sound, so it was possibly an attempt at 'Marina'. Or else, as that eloquent thread of her legend has always claimed, a reference to her original Nahuatl name, 'Malinalli', or its Mayan equivalent, 'Malina'.

This then is how her most enduring name evolved, through a muddled, mispronounced and misheard fusion of Spanish and Nahuatl. It is an appropriate process for such a woman, a process poignantly symbolic of the complexities of a life lived among different peoples, different language groups.

Diaz tells us also that because the people who watched them pass identified Cortés so closely with Malinche, they called him by her name: 'Malinche' or 'Lord Malinche'. It is a curious reversal of the usual conventions. To think that this most famous of conquerors, whose own concise Spanish name has thundered so relentlessly through history, was known initially among the people he had come to conquer by the name of his concubine, a captive woman, a slave: Malinche.

Malinche and Cortés

When I think about the past and the famous people who lived it, it is the small and intimate details I want to know: the way they moved, their gestures, the sound of their voices, their smells, how they made love, gave birth, and died. Initial impressions are particularly precious for their raw and intricate detail, like that first detailed description of the Spaniards in The Florentine Codex. 'They were very white. Their eyes were like chalk . . .'

But no one ever really tells us how Malinche looked. Not Cortés, who made only two fleeting references to her in his correspondence, and only once by name. Not even Bernal Diaz, whose description of her is disappointingly general. 'A woman of great being,' he says, 'a woman of fine appearance.' It is something, but not much, to go on. She is always assumed to have been a handsome woman. Bernal Diaz clearly thought she was, and his opinion is supported by the fact that when she first joined their company at Potonchan, Cortés gave her to his favourite, Puertocarrero, who despite his youth was the most illustrious member of the expedition in terms of social rank.

Diaz said that when Moctezuma's first emissaries appeared at Veracruz they brought with them a group of painters who quickly set about recording likenesses of Cortés and his expedition. They drew everything, he said, 'the ships, sails, and horses, Doña Marina and Aguilar, and even the two greyhounds . . . and the drawings were taken to Moctezuma'. But these extraordinary works have never been recovered. They were probably destroyed during the battle for Tenochtitlan.

All the portraits I have ever seen of Malinche have been the imaginings of men who did not know her, who never set eyes on her. I have seen her naked and forlorn beneath the stairs in the College of San Ildefonso in Mexico City, observant and watchful on the walls of the National Palace, modest and comely as the Botticelli Venus in that old engraving of the meeting at Potonchan.

There are many other representations of Malinche. In Mexico, around the middle of the sixteenth century, indigenous histories of the Conquest began slowly to emerge. They go by wonderful names: the Florentine Codex, the Tepetlan Codex, the *Lienzo de Tlaxcala*, and so on. Each one is named for the town or state of its origin, or in the case of the Florentine Codex, the Italian city Florence, where it is now housed.

In these beautiful and important painted books, Malinche is a constant figure. She is usually dressed simply in an embroidered *huipil*. Sometimes her hair is caught up at the temples in two little horns, a style still favoured by Mayan women throughout Meso America. In other illustrations she wears it long and loose, according to the conventions for an unmarried woman of her time, and a small tongue-like scroll usually floats above her head to symbolise her speech. She is always central to the illustrations in which she appears. The Spaniards stand to one side of her, Amerindian dignitaries and warriors to the other. Often she is shown receiving gifts of turkeys and blankets, or giving religious instruction.

Her placement in the illustrations, even her size, which is frequently larger than the men on either side of her, is powerful, wordless testimony to her visibility and her supreme importance to those who saw her pass. But as portraits they reveal nothing of her individual features, her posture, her expression. She is portrayed with a doll-like anonymity, a formulaic beauty.

MALINCHE INTERPRETS FOR CORTÉS AND
RECEIVES GIFTS FROM THE TLAXCLANS
(from Lienzo de Tlaxcala, c. 1550)

MALINCHE SLEEPS DURING THE JOURNEY TO TENOCHTITLAN

(from Lienzo de Tlaxcala, c. 1550)

MALINCHE BESIDE CORTÉS AT BAPTISM

OF TLAXCALAN NOBLES

(from Lienzo de Tlaxcala, c. 1550)

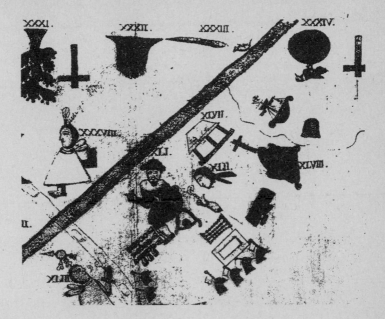

MALINCHE IS OFFERED GIFTS OF BLANKETS

AND TURKEYS, DETAIL

(from Tepetlan Codex, c. 1550)

When I think about Malinche now, I hold to my own image of her, the way she might have looked in Potonchan on the eve of the Conquest. Around eighteen years of age, copper skin, hawk nose, epicanthic eyes, pellucid black hair. Around her neck she wears a string of golden beads, and on her feet a pair of rubber sandals, in the contemporary fashion of the tropical south. I see her standing there in an embroidered *huipil,* dark eyes watching carefully. She is small and erect, elegant and astute. She has a fine sense of irony, and when she laughs she throws her head back, like the iguana seller in Jaltipan.

In the case of Hernan Cortés, however, Bernal Diaz has left a clear and detailed description of his commander. 'He was of good stature,' Diaz said, 'and figure well-proportioned and robust . . . and in his eyes and expression there was something kindly but on the other hand grave.' His beard was rather dark and scanty but 'he had a deep chest and well-shaped shoulders, and was lean and with very little belly, and slightly bow-legged, with the legs and thighs well set-on'.

Diaz recalled a scar near Cortés's underlip, from a wound he had received 'in one of his knife fights over women', and he said that, if one looked hard at the scar, 'he was inclined to cover it up more with his beard'. It is an interesting comment that suggests a certain vain self-consciousness. There are abundant visual studies too, as we would expect with such a rich and important public man. His likeness was captured, in paint and metal and words, by numerous observers, and they go by edifying titles such as *Valiant Cortés*, in which he gazes heaven-ward, hands joined in prayer like a medieval saint, pious in shining black armour.

Fortunately at least one sharp-eyed artist more concerned with accuracy than flattery has left a portrait usually considered to be a true likeness. He was a German painter called Christoph Weiditz. He happened to be in residence at the Spanish Court in 1528, and he made a series of watercolour studies of the indigenous Mexicans who accompanied Cortés on his trium-phant return to his homeland that year. Weiditz also took the opportunity to strike a medallion of the conqueror himself. It is housed now in Berlin's Staatliche Museum, and the face that looks out is free of the contrived, sanctimonious air of so many other portraits of Cortés. It is neither ugly nor particularly handsome or distinguished. The metallic eyes are sightless, the face and nose are long, the mouth is small and partially obscured by a pendulous moustache. The beard is cut across in a straight line, the hair falls evenly almost to the shoulders and it has been trimmed with the same blunt, geometric precision. He wears an unadorned doublet and a flat beret-like cap, made of velvet perhaps. What appears to be a scar runs across his lower right cheek in a diagonal line.

MEDALLION OF HERNAN CORTÉS BY
CHRISTOPH WEIDITZ, 1529
(from collection of Staatliche Museum, Berlin)

It is an ordinary face but the set of that small hard mouth suggests a shrewd and emphatic nature. Or perhaps we read what we believe into such a portrait. We see the familiar name inscribed around the medallion's rim, 'Don Ferdinando Cortés', with the not uncommon transposition of 'F' for 'H' in his Christian name. We know that name and something of its owner's exploits. Perhaps it is that knowledge which makes this face seem so implacable.

What of the man himself? From his letters we can see the comparisons he made as he sought to comprehend and describe the exotic world of the Americas. His own country, Spain, had only just emerged from eight centuries of Islamic domination, and its influence is clear in his descriptions. When he gazed on the temples and pyramids of the Maya, the Totonac and the Aztecs, he saw 'mosques'. The clothes people wore looked to him like Arabic clothes. 'Large highly coloured yashmaks,' he called them, 'thin mantles which are decorated in Moorish fashion.'

Cortés had been born into the lesser nobility. He was, like Bernal Diaz, an *hidalgo*: literally in Spanish 'the son of somebody'. He had studied for a time at the University of Salamanca, but in 1504, before his studies were complete, he had sailed for the West Indies and settled in Cuba. The stirring speeches he made to his men at the most critical moments were littered with allusions to Caesar and Aristotle, and those frequent references convinced many of his contemporaries that he was a classical scholar.

The historian J. H. Elliott believes that while Cortés was probably quite well read, more importantly he had 'a quick ear and eye for the arresting phrase, and a genius for putting it to good use'. Elliott observes that although Cortés, like most of his compatriots, believed in the power of 'fortune's wheel', he believed that this almighty wheel could be overcome by force of will. It was an attitude unusual for its time, one that Elliott likens to that of Machiavelli. To illustrate this point he tells a striking anecdote.

After the fall of Tenochtitlan, when jousting at the ring with some of his men, Cortés selected as his emblem a wheel of fortune and a figure of a man with a hammer in one hand and a nail in the other. He devised a motto to accompany this design, which read: 'I shall hammer in the nail when I see that there is nothing more to possess.'

Cortés was not a renowned navigator and explorer like his Portuguese contemporary, Ferdinand Magellan, or his Italian predecessor, Columbus. He was a notary who raised a private expedition and set out from Cuba. He had the governor's permission to proceed along the mainland coast as far as San Juan de Ulua, then turn back just as Juan de Grijalva had done the previous year. But he disobeyed his orders and went further. He made an unexpected conquest that changed the shape of our world forever.

Certain times and certain deeds require the invention of new words and new expressions. In 1519 when Cortés and his companions sailed from Cuba they were known simply by their trades and professions. They were notaries, blacksmiths, carpenters, musicians, physicians and soldiers, and their mission was to explore and trade along the mainland coast. But in view of what happened on that journey, Spaniards were inspired to coin a new word for these redoubtable adventurers and those who came after them: *conquistador*. In 1519 when Cortés arrived on the coast of Mexico it had not yet been invented, but soon would be.

Malinche's sexual liaison with Cortés must have begun around the middle of 1519. Earlier that year, in Potonchan, Cortés had allotted her to his young and aristocratic friend, Hernando Alonso Puertocarrero. We have no way of knowing what kind of relationship Malinche had enjoyed or endured with this man in the intervening months, for these are things that history does not speak about.

Presumably, however, like the other women who had gone with her to the Spaniards, she gathered wood and carried water, tended Puertocarrero's fire, prepared his food, and shared his sleeping mat with him, when she was called upon to do so. In July, while the expedition was still encamped at Veracruz, Puertocarrero left for Spain. He went as Cortés's emissary, bearing despatches and treasure for King Charles. 'And when Puertocarrero returned to Spain,' Bernal Diaz tells us, 'doña Marina lived with Cortés to whom she bore a son called don Martin Cortés.'

We know little of Malinche's sexual history, but quite a lot about Cortés's for long before Malinche was ever heard of, he was already notorious for his promiscuity, and long after her death his notoriety would continue. In Cuba, for example, where he had lived for fifteen years before launching his expedition to the mainland, there had been persistent scandal.

There was an incident in which he fell from a wall one night while abroad on some illicit sexual adventure.

When he married his first wife, Beatriz Juarez de Marcaida, it was amid controversy, possibly under duress, for it appears he had compromised her reputation with his behaviour. In Mexico, after the Conquest, Cortés's womanising would continue to be the subject of intense and constant colonial gossip, and even the focus of judicial enquiry.

Bernal Diaz referred to all this in his memoirs. He admired his commander, but he was no fool and he saw his faults too. He admitted that he had heard Cortés was 'dissolute with women' and 'addicted to women in excess, and jealous in guarding his own'.

So what was Malinche, exactly, to Cortés? Lover, mistress, concubine, whore? She has been called each and every one of these terms throughout the centuries since her death, depending on the bias of the speaker or the writer. You could consider all these words with all their various nuances, as I have, constantly. You could weigh them up in light of whatever paltry evidence you can discover, turn them over and over in your mind, and still not know which one comes closest to the truth.

Malinche and Cortés did not marry, and during the years when he is believed to have been with her, he was constantly involved with other women, both Spanish and Amerindian. This may not, in itself, have concerned her. She had been raised in the polygamous Mayan world of Potonchan, and monogamy was a state she had no reason to expect, or even desire, with any man. But the depth of their feelings for each other remains hidden from us.

Their liaison may have been a genuine attachment or just as easily a 'marriage' of convenience for both. At worst, from Malinche's point of view, she may have pined for his devotion, while he thought little of her.

Neither of them left any record of their sentiments towards the other, however. Therefore, all we can say for certain is that after July 1519 and throughout the next four years, Cortés and Malinche were frequently together, and seen to be together. And that in 1522 she bore a son to him, a child he called Martin, after his beloved father back in Spain.

We People Here

From Jalapa I turned south as Malinche had done, and made my way in local buses down winding, dangerous mountain roads toward the state of Tlaxcala. Here in this high, windswept landscape, the Spaniards' journey turned to nightmare as they struggled through an icy mountain pass into a desert of volcanic ash and sand, and looked out on Mexico's highest peak.

It already had an elegant name, in Nahuatl, Citlaltepetl, 'Star Mountain'. But the naming and re-naming of places, and people, is an essential ritual of possession. So with the usual arrogance of invaders, the Spaniards christened it in their own language: Orizaba.

They had first observed this great volcano some months earlier as they sailed along the coast from Potonchan to Veracruz. It had puzzled them as it hovered there above the hot luxuriant coastal plain, incongruous in its cape of ice and snow. 'It is so white we think it to be covered in snow,' Cortés wrote, 'but as we have not seen it very clearly . . . and because this region is so hot, we cannot be certain that it is.'

That night they felt Orizaba's frigid breath and almost perished in a hailstorm on its slopes. They had nothing but their armour for covering, and they knew for certain now, to their misery, that it was indeed snow they had seen in the distance.

From certain high points in the state of Tlaxcala it is possible, in the early morning when the skies are clear, to see four volcanoes at once. To the east, you can just make out the glittering pinnacle of Orizaba, to the west the snowcapped cones of Popocatepetl and Iztaccihuatl look down toward Mexico City. But in the foreground there is another tall and graceful peak. In winter its sloping flanks are covered with snow, in summer they are brilliantly green.

It was once called 'Matlecueye' in honour of the jade-skirted wife of the rain god, but these days it is known as La Malinche. Malinche herself would have seen this mountain. She would have walked beneath its slopes as she made her way down from Jalapa toward Tenochtitlan, never dreaming that one day the volcano would bear her name.

It is not clear how or when its name changed. Late in the sixteenth century a Spanish monk who had grown up among the ruins of Tenochtitlan, and was a fine Nahuatl speaker, still referred to it in his writings as Matlecueye. He said it meant 'she of the olive-green skirt . . . because of the fresh greenness and green woods that cover the slopes of this mountain'. But he also noted that many Spaniards had begun to call it 'Doña Mencia', which is curious. It suggests that in the early years following the Conquest this graceful volcano had borne another woman's name for a time. Who was this 'Doña Mencia'? Whose mother, whose daughter, or long-forgotten lover?

...

I took a bus from the northern side of La Malinche, along a dusty mountain road, toward the tiny village of San Andres Ahuahuaztepec. As we neared the village the other passengers pointed to the surrounding hillsides. They told me that if I searched carefully I might find tiny jagged shards of flint and obsidian. Relics, they said, of a great battle their ancestors had once fought there against the Spaniards.

San Andres, like every other town in Mexico, is laid out around a central plaza with a church at one end. The church in San Andres is small but its exterior, overlain with glazed tiles in blue and white, is intricate and beautiful. It was late afternoon when I arrived, the wooden pews were filled with people, the altar glowed with candles, and a woman's voice was leading the rosary. I couldn't see her among the cluster of worshippers, some kneeling, some sitting. But from time to time I heard her calling softly, *Salve Maria, Santa Maria*, from somewhere in the front of the church.

When the rosary finished, people began leaving quietly, and as they did I made my way toward the front. An elderly woman was adjusting the flowers and after she had crossed herself and genuflected, I approached her. 'Perdoname, señora,' I whispered, 'I believe there is a painting here, somewhere.' I explained what I was looking for.

'Yes,' she said, 'I'll show you.'

The sacristy was to the left of the altar. She ushered me inside. I saw a polished wooden cabinet with priest's vestments arranged methodically on hangers, and, beside it on the wall, a cracked and faded study of four figures: three men, one woman.

I moved closer and saw that their names were painted carefully beneath them: 'Hernan Cortés', 'Saint Andrew', to whom the village had been dedicated after the Conquest, and 'Xicontencatl', the sixteenth-century lord of Tlaxcala. The woman at the painting's centre, between the conqueror, the saint and the native lord, was Malinche. Her face had been finely drawn, her hair was coiled in a spindle across her temples, and she wore a luxurious *huipil* trimmed with feathers. A quiver of arrows was slung across her right shoulder, and beneath her feet lay a small crown of plumes. Her Spanish name, 'doña Marina', was inscribed below her feet.

I was so intent on the painting, I had almost forgotten the woman beside me. She stood there waiting, with a spray of bougainvillea in her hands. 'It's beautiful,' I murmured.

She nodded. 'It was painted early in the eighteenth century.'

I asked her if she knew who had painted it. 'Several artists, I believe, people from here in the village,' she replied.

She thought for a moment. 'Which direction have you come from?' she asked.

'From Jalapa,' I told her. 'And Veracruz before that.'

'So you have not come through San Pedro?' I must have looked puzzled.

'San Pedro Tlacotepec. It's south of the volcano,' she said by way of explanation. 'It's just that I have heard there is another one like this, over there, in San Pedro.'

We walked to the church door and stood looking out in the direction of La Malinche.

'Malinche has always been venerated, here in Tlaxcala,' the

woman told me, in confidential tones. 'But perhaps we have been punished for this. People say that is why all our young men leave. They go to the capital, or to the north, or even worse, to the United States. Well, you know, that's how it is throughout Mexico.' She turned toward the volcano and sighed, 'But around here, people say that it's because of Malinche, because of our attachment to her. That's why we are losing them. It's a curse, they say . . . the allure of foreign things.'

Tlaxcala is now the smallest state in the republic of Mexico but in September 1519, when the Spaniards entered its mountainous reaches, it was an independent nation. During the previous century almost all its neighbouring city states had succumbed to Culua-Mexica domination. Only Tlaxcala and nearby Huejotzingo, now a district of the present state of Tlaxcala, had remained autonomous. They lay together just a few days march from Tenochtitlan, and in spite of their perilous geography they had resisted the aggression of Moctezuma's empire with a ferocity rare in central Mexico.

The alliance Cortés forged with these two powerful city states was fundamental to his victory. It expanded his forces by tens of thousands. It brought him battle-hardened warriors equipped with intimate knowledge and murderous hatred of the Culua-Mexica. Without the assistance of Tlaxcala and Huejotzingo, Cortés and his men would probably have perished before they laid eyes on Tenochtitlan.

As allies the Tlaxcalans were not easily won. No nation as courageously defiant, as bellicose and independent as they were, would have welcomed this foreign army encroaching on their territory. Initially a series of battles were fought on the slopes around San Andres Ahuahuaztepec — battles so ferocious, Bernal Diaz said later, that the Spaniards were in a desperate state, marooned on an icy mountainside in Tlaxcala, badly wounded, panic-stricken. Some became openly mutinous. It was at this dangerous moment that the alliances with Tlaxcala and Huejotzingo were forged.

The precise manner in which the alliances came about is hidden from us, but Bernal Diaz tells us that Malinche went with Cortés to negotiate with the Tlaxcalan leaders, who were, like the Culua-Mexica, Nahuatl speakers. Diaz was not present at this meeting, so we do not know precisely what Malinche said to them, what deals were struck, what mutually advantageous arrangements were entered into. We do know, however, that the Tlaxcalans too had been severely injured in their battles with the Spaniards. The unfamiliar explosive weapons used against them had caused terrifying wounds and multiple deaths, unprecedented in Tlaxcalan military experience. In the face of this they must have been persuaded that a coalition with the Spaniards against Tenochtitlan would be to their benefit.

Just two weeks later, as if to cement their alliance, Spaniards fell upon the nearby city of Cholula, which was Tlaxcala's enemy, and massacred thousands of its residents. The massacre at Cholula caused outrage among Spanish opponents of the Conquest when they learned about it later. The tireless Dominican polemicist, Bartolome de las Casas, denounced it forever as the atrocity it was. Cholula became a controversy that

Cortés would be obliged to defend himself against for the rest of his days.

Bernal Diaz del Castillo always supported Cortés's story that the Spaniards had turned on Cholula in self-defence. He claimed in his memoirs that an old Cholulan woman had taken a liking to Malinche, and while enticing her to marry her son, the old woman had warned Malinche of an impending Cholulan attack on the Spaniards. Diaz said that Malinche went straight to Cortés to warn him of the danger, and that was when the Spaniards decided to turn on Cholula. This alleged plot was always Cortés's justification for Cholula.

Bartolome de las Casas refused to believe the story of the old woman and Malinche and the so-called conspiracy. He decried the Cholula massacre as an act of terror against innocent people, which it undoubtedly was. Cholula was not a military strong-hold but a peaceable city whose citizens had recently yielded to Culua-Mexica domination. Their only crime was to be rather too vulnerable enemies of Tlaxcala. It seems probable that the massacre at Cholula was the price, or part of the price, that Malinche negotiated on Cortés's behalf, in return for Tlaxcalan loyalty.

Forty years later the people of Tlaxcala prepared their own painted history of the Conquest. The *Lienzo de Tlaxcala*, as it is called, was not intended as a work of art, nor a history for its own sake. It was a pictorial account of services rendered to the Spaniards by the Tlaxcalans during and after the Conquest. It formed the basis of their request for special privileges from the Spanish Crown.

The original *Lienzo* vanished long ago. Perhaps it is lying forgotten in the basement of some great museum in Madrid or Vienna, the way Moctezuma's famous headdress was until the eighteenth century, when it turned up in a Tyrolean castle. But several copies of the *Lienzo* have survived, and Malinche appears in almost half of the forty-eight meticulous illustrations.

We see her watching as Cortés greets the lord of Tlaxcala, Xicontecatl; we see her present at his baptism. We see her sleeping with her face resting on her hand; we see her carrying a shield and giving Christian instruction to the Tlaxcalans. The pictures form a powerful, wordless testimony to her critical importance in Tlaxcalan eyes.

However it came about, whatever Malinche's part in fashioning this essential alliance, peace was achieved. 'And we gave great thanks to God,' Diaz said, 'for at that moment we were lean, weary and unhappy about this war, of which we could neither see nor forecast the end.'

In 1560 the men of Huejotzingo wrote a famous letter to King Phillip of Spain. Like the *Lienzo de Tlaxcala* it was an inventory of the assistance they had supplied to Cortés during the wars of Conquest. In return for that critical assistance, certain privileges were now requested.

In their letter the Huejotzingans were at pains to point out that while the Tlaxcalans had initially fought against the Spaniards, they had received Cortés and his men very gladly from the first. 'We embraced them,' the Huejotzingans wrote. 'We saluted them with many tears though we were not acquainted with them . . . nowhere did we attack them . . . we began to feed them and serve them . . . And when they began their conquest and war-making, then also we prepared ourselves well to aid them . . . we helped them not only in warfare . . . it was we who worked so that they could conquer the Mexica with boats.'

The Huejotzingans went on to detail the years of military support they had given to the Spaniards as together they travelled the length and breadth of Meso America, as far south as Nicaragua, as far north as California, claiming new territory for the Spanish empire.

'And when they conquered the Mexica and all belonging to them,' the Huejotzingans wrote, 'we never abandoned them or left them behind in it. And when they went to conquer Michoacan, Jalisco, and Colhuacan and at Panuco and Oaxaca, Tehuantepec and Guatemala, and all over New Spain here where they conquered and made war until they finished their conquests, we never abandoned them. In this we do not lie, for the conquerors themselves know it.'

Popular history has chosen to ignore these great indigenous alliances. The myth of the easy European conquest of Mexico, like the myth of the easy European conquest of Australia, or worse, no conquest at all — *terra nullius*, empty land — has long been enshrined in our understanding of these momentous events.

If we are surprised or shocked to learn about the Tlaxcalan and Huejotzingan contribution to the Conquest perhaps it is due in part to our incapacity to comprehend diversity among non-Europeans. We know very well that Italians are not the same as Scots or Germans, that to be Irish is to be different from

English. But we appear to have difficulty understanding that indigenous Americans, Africans, Australians, are not, and never were, one indistinct, amorphous people. We want them to be 'indians', 'natives', or in the case of Mexico, we want them all to be 'Aztecs'. It would be so much easier for our understanding of the Conquest if they were.

The reality is that the Tlaxcalans and Huejotzingans fought with Cortés, and that without their support he and his men may well have perished. Like Malinche, the Tlaxcalans owed no allegiance to the Culua-Mexica, and there was nothing treacherous in their conduct. The Conquest was to them just one more episode in their long-running war with Tenochtitlan.

It seems clear that before the coming of the Spaniards the inhabitants of what we now call Mexico had no collective sense of identity, any more than did the peoples of Italy, or the British Isles, or the Balkans, or Australia at that time. They did not need a collective sense of themselves because they knew precisely who they were. They were the Maya, the Culua-Mexica, the Totonac, the Tlaxcalans, the Huejotzingans, the Cholulans.

Therefore, no equivalent existed in their languages for the generic label, 'indian', that Europe pressed on them after 1492 when Columbus made his famous error. Nor did one exist for the several other words we have since coined to describe them: 'Amerindian', 'American', 'Native American'. To the Maya, the Tlaxcalans, the Huejotzingas, the Culua-Mexica, these words with their sense of 'one people' would have meant nothing. They knew what European empire-builders in the Americas, in Africa, and later, in Australia, have never understood: that the indigenous peoples of those continents were never all one and the same people.

Late in the 1980s the historian James Lockhart became a visiting scholar at my old university and I made a special trip to the city to hear him speak at a seminar one hot, autumn afternoon. He explained how he and his colleagues in Mexico City had stumbled upon a forgotten cache of legal documents written in Nahuatl in the years immediately following the Conquest.

The papers were a record of legal battles, he discovered, small intriguing neighbourhood disputes concerning donkeys, household implements and parcels of land, altercations conducted and documented throughout those post-Conquest years. Lockhart described how with the discovery of those documents he became an accidental student, later a scholar, of Nahuatl.

James Lockhart has searched painstakingly and unsuccessfully among those documents and also among the more formal Nahuatl histories of the Conquest such as the Florentine Codex, for a collective Nahuatl expression for the indigenous peoples of Mexico. He concludes that their pre-Conquest world was too strongly and persistently divided by 'micro-patriotism' to have conceived of such an expression.

Even in the aftermath of the Conquest that collective sense, he believes, was slow to evolve. The appearance on the horizon of the Spaniards does not seem to have inspired the creation of such a term, as we might have expected. When the Spaniards arrived, Lockhart believes, they entered the scene as just one more player, one more antagonist, in a complex, warlike jigsaw.

The closest Lockhart has found to an expression of collective consciousness occurs some forty years after the Conquest, in Book 12 of the Florentine Codex. The expression is *'nican tlaca'*, which Lockhart translates as 'here people'.

This rare and poignant expression, *nican tlaca,* occurs only three times in the lengthy Florentine Codex. It is significant for Malinche's story that the first time it appears is in relation to her. *'Ce cioatl nican titlaca'*, the Florentine Codex calls her: 'A woman, one of us people here.'

It is as if on seeing Malinche among the strangers, the Castillian people, *Caxtillan tlaca,* that the first tremor of collective identity, the first suggestion of a 'we', as opposed to a 'they', begins to stir in Culua-Mexica minds.

⚜

Popocatepetl and Iztaccihuatl, the twin volcanoes, sit poised on the edge of Tlaxcala, looking down toward what is now the outer sprawl of Mexico City. Legend has it that they are lovers — volcano lovers. They are also the ancient guardians of Mexico City. For centuries they have watched as wave after wave of nomads have wandered down from the northern deserts into the fertile Valley of Mexico, and have been seduced by its beauty, just as the *Azteca,* the people of heron place, were seduced in the early years of the twelfth century.

The Spaniards, of course, came from a different direction. They arrived from the east, a new kind of barbarian, and as they made their way down through Tlaxcala, they observed the two magnificent mountains with great interest. They were especially

intrigued by Popocatepetl, which was in a highly active phase
that year, and they were puzzled by the presence of the icy peaks
in such a hot climate, just as they had been several months earlier
as they gazed from their ships toward Mount Orizaba.

'From one of them which is the higher,' Cortés later wrote to
the king, 'there appears often by day and night a great cloud of
smoke as big as a house which goes straight as an arrow up into
the clouds and seems to come out with such force.' In his letters
at this time he seems increasingly intrigued by the dangerous
beauty and incongruousness of Mexico, this land of heat and ice
and snow and earthquake.

None of the Spaniards, Bernal Diaz said, had ever seen an
active volcano before, so Cortés sent his friend, Diego de Ordaz,
with a small group of men to climb Popocatepetl. Ordaz reached
almost to the rim of Popocatepetl's crater, and as it rumbled and
shook and hurled out stones and ash in a small eruption, he
became the first European to look on Tenochtitlan.

Bernal Diaz remembered Diego de Ordaz later as 'brave
and judicious . . . with something of a stammer'. When Ordaz
climbed back down from Popcatepetl, he presumably stammered
out his excited account of what he had seen from the crater. It
was several days before Malinche and Cortés, and all the others,
struggled up through the snowy mountain pass between the two
volcanoes and saw Tenochtitlan for themselves.

'It was like the enchantments they tell of in the legend of
Amadis,' Diaz said, referring to his favourite tale of chivalry.
'And some of our soldiers even asked whether the things that we
saw were not a dream . . . seeing things as we did that had never

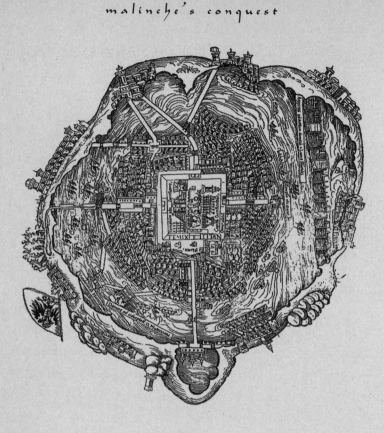

SIXTEENTH-CENTURY EUROPEAN MAP OF TENOCHTITLAN

(first published in Hernan Cortés's Second Letter,

in Nuremburg, 1524)

been heard of or seen before, not even dreamed about.'

His response has become famous. It has reverberated through history like a requiem, a final anthem to the wondrous city that the Spaniards and their Tlaxcalan allies would destroy within two years.

When the Shield was Laid Down

On the Sunday morning after my return to the capital I climbed the hill above the Basilica of Our Lady of Guadalupe to look out for Filomena Alvarado. It was around ten o'clock when I saw her tiny black-robed figure emerge from the crowd of amulet-sellers massed around the edge of the square with their scapulas and rosaries and holy pictures. I hurried down to meet her. 'There is a pilgrimage this morning, from Chiapas,' she told me.

The basilica's entrance was already overflowing with people when the procession appeared from across the square. The Mayan pilgrims had travelled up from the south in their borrowed trucks and old buses. They had come from their traditional villages around Palenque, San Cristobal de las Casas and Amatenango, and they walked past us gravely, their faces intense and resolute beneath a banner of Our Lady of Guadalupe.

Their bishop, Samuel Ruiz, followed behind them in full regalia, with his mitre and crook and his satin cope. He had come despite the death threats of the cattle barons, who resented his involvement in this increasingly violent dispute. They were determined never to relinquish the traditional Mayan lands they had appropriated for their own use. But Bishop Ruiz had a famous precedent for his loyalty to the Maya. The first bishop of Chiapas had been Bartolome de las Casas, the Dominican priest who had condemned the massacre at Cholula five centuries earlier.

We watched the pilgrims disappear slowly inside for a mass dedicated to their struggle for land rights, and as the crowd closed behind them, we turned and climbed the stone steps cut into the cliff above the basilica. I told Filomena I had seen the temples and pyramids of Palenque again, and had found them just as haunting as I remembered from my first visit. She was in a melancholy mood that morning.

'Have you noticed,' she said as we climbed, 'the way that in Mexico we romanticise our indigenous past but ignore the indigenous present. We praise the ancient Maya, but we repudiate their descendants living among us now. To acknowledge their existence and their humanity might imply certain obligations, such as returning their traditional lands to them.'

'Yes,' I said, 'I've noticed all this. But Mexico is not alone in that hypocrisy.'

'What do you mean?'

'Well, I grew up believing that the Indigenous people of Tasmania were extinct, that they had all died, or been murdered, during European colonisation. When I was a child this was something we were taught in Australian schools. Then, one day, I think it was about eight years ago, I heard a Tasmanian Aboriginal woman speaking. She was angry. "We are still here!"

she said. "We have endured in spite of everything you have done to us."'

Filomena was listening carefully.

'I saw how important it was for her to stand up, to be seen to be alive. She showed me that the indecent haste with which her people had been consigned to the past was another form of extermination, a way of excluding them from the present. What she said made a profound impression on me.'

The hill on which we stood had been a sacred place for centuries. Long before the Spanish came it had belonged to another great maternal spirit. Tonantzin, 'Our Mother', the Culua-Mexica called her. From the crest of what was once her shrine, we could see Mexico City spread out across the lake bed, trapped within its fortress of mountains. A line of jets was making its approach to the airport, and above the foothills to the east, we could just make out the high snowy peak of Iztaccihuatl. But Popocateptl was lost amid the brown pall of smog that chokes this city.

'The pass is up there somewhere, between the volcanoes,' Filomena said, shading her eyes against the morning glare as she gazed toward Iztaccihuatl. 'That's the way they came, through the Paso de Cortés. But of course it's impossible to see it now, through all this *contaminación*.'

Mexico City was once the most beautiful city in the Americas: 'Mexico-Tenochtitlan . . . among the reeds and the rushes . . . standing in the midst of waters', according to an old Culua-Mexica song that survived the Conquest.

The city has surrendered its beauty now to earthquake and

pollution, and there is a sense that you could slide into catastrophe at any moment among the leaning palaces and churches, beneath the glowering, livid sky and the constant showers of ash from Popocatepetl.

In 1519, however, when Bernal Diaz saw its antecedent, Tenochtitlan, glistening on its island in the middle of Lake Texcoco, it was a miracle of elegant design compared to the European cities he had known. With its population of around 200 000 people, it was larger by far than most European cities at that time, and more orderly, with its straight clean streets and canals. Most amazing of all was the great stone aqueduct, which brought fresh water into the city from the woodlands of Chapultepec, while a constant flotilla of canoes carried human waste silently and efficiently away to the cultivation fields of Xochimilco.

But after its destruction in 1521, the city lay in smouldering ruins for many months until rebuilding commenced, a task Cortés took very seriously. He seems to have been intent on recapturing, in European terms, something of the beauty which he had seen and lost. Tenochtitlan had been his vainglory, his proof to the world outside, to Europe, that he had truly won a magnificent empire.

So after the horror, the city began slowly to rise again. In their letters home the Spaniards referred to it as *Temystitan-Mexico,* in a mangled echo of its former title, but gradually that echo evolved into 'Mexico City'. The grace and elegance of its fine architecture and urban planning were admired by visitors for centuries to come.

The elegant buildings, the cloisters and plazas are all still there in the old quarter. The ruined temples of Huitzilopochtli and Tlaloc have been miraculously uncovered, and their stones lie beside the cathedral in the central plaza for all to see. But the metropolis of modern Mexico City hovers constantly on the brink of a disastrous water shortage, and the old song extolling the beauty of this place in 'water's midst' seems a bitter jest.

It was 8 November 1519 when Cortés and Malinche, the Spaniards and their allies, the Tlaxcalans and the Huejotzingans, finally emerged from the mountains. As they made their way across the principal causeway toward the city in the lake, the people of Tenochtitlan came out to watch them.

They saw, for the first time, the horses with their clattering hooves and bridle bells. 'The bells resounded . . .' their descendants remembered later '. . . there was a pounding as if stones were cast at one.' They saw the terrifying mastiffs and greyhounds that had accompanied the expedition: 'each one came continually panting', the swordsmen: 'their iron swords went flashing', and the arquebuses: 'they each exploded, they each crackled, were discharged, thundered, disgorged'.

The standard bearer, but more particularly, his banner, attracted close attention: 'He came continually shaking it . . . making it circle . . . it came rising like a warrior . . . it came twisting and filling itself out.' Then the watchers on the causeway saw Cortés himself, 'the commander, the *tlacateccatl*, the battle ruler', and beside him, his foot soldiers, men like Bernal Diaz, 'his brave warriors . . . the strong ones, the intrepid ones'.

Finally, and most ominously, they saw their long-standing

enemies from Tlaxcala and Huejotzingo. They had come 'arrayed for war . . . with their knees bent, loosing cries, loosing shrieks while striking their mouths with their hands, singing the Tocuillan song'.

This account of the strange procession across the causeway first appeared in The Florentine Codex around 1555, some thirty-six years after the event. The Nahuatl scholars who prepared it were very young men, too young to have witnessed the events they described, so their account must have come from their parents and grandparents. Although it is remembered and imagined, rather than experienced directly, their words are as candid and painstaking as those of Bernal Diaz. They reflect the wonderment of people who were seeing amazing things for the first time, for whom nothing could be taken for granted.

The Florentine Codex does not mention Malinche at this point. She was probably just one of the anonymous women and African slaves who walked with the soldiers in the horses' dust. But Bernal Diaz tells us that at a certain interval on the causeway, their thundering, clanging, whooping cavalcade suddenly paused while Malinche explained that Moctezuma was on his way to meet them.

By now they could see the lofty temples and pyramids of Tenochtitlan quite clearly, painted brilliantly in green and red, turquoise and yellow. As they surveyed this extraordinary scene, a magnificent litter appeared in the distance, coming toward them along the causeway from the city. It came to rest not far from where they stood waiting, and Moctezuma descended. He walked with great ceremony toward them, while his attendants

MALINCHE AND MOCTEZUMA ON CAUSEWAY
TO TENOCHTITLAN
(from Lienzo de Tlaxcala, c. 1550)

held above him a canopy of quetzal feathers, gold and silver thread and pearls.

Diaz was amazed by the ruler's sumptuous dress and noted that his sandals were made of gold, with the upper layers encrusted with precious stones. He also made a careful study of the Culua-Mexica ruler's face and figure. 'The great lord Moctezuma,' he recalled later, 'was about forty years old, of good height, well-proportioned, spare and slight, and not very dark, though of the usual Indian complexion . . . He had fine eyes and in his appearance and manner could express geniality or, when necessary, a serious composure.'

Diaz noticed that none of Moctezuma's attendants looked him in the face. 'All kept their eyes lowered most reverently except those four lords, his nephews, who were supporting him.' The Spaniards suffered no such inhibitions, a fact the Florentine Codex later recalled with disapproval.

They stared at him, it records, 'each of them giving him a close look . . . they would start along, walking, then mount, then dismount again in order to see him'. When suddenly Cortés attempted to embrace Moctezuma, his noble attendants grasped the Spaniard by the arms and prevented him from doing so, 'for they considered this an indignity'.

Shortly after recounting this tense and inauspicious beginning, the Florentine Codex makes its first reference to Malinche's presence on the causeway. When calm had been restored, it tells us, Moctezuma made a welcoming speech to the Spaniards, and 'Malintzin reported it to him, interpreting it for him'.

She must have stepped forward, like an actor taking her place at centre stage. 'And when the Marques [Cortés] had heard what Moteucçoma [Moctezuma] had said,' the Codex continues, 'he spoke to Malintzin in return, replying in his babbling tongue.' Here we have the customary Nahuatl disdain for other people's language: Cortés was a 'babbler', he spoke a barbaric tongue.

The Codex makes no mention at this point of Geronimo de Aguilar, as if both he and his hard-won Mayan had already faded from the interpreting chain. Does this mean Malinche was by this time well-conversant in Spanish? It is highly likely. For nine months now she had lived among Spaniards; sufficient time for a woman of her linguistic abilities to acquire a new tongue.

Moctezuma knew about Malinche. Between April and that day in November 1519 he had constantly received intelligence reports about the Spaniards and all who travelled with them. The court painters who went with his emissaries to the coast to meet Cortés had provided him with paintings of the newcomers, and in these he had seen Cortés, his horses and dogs, his soldiers, and the woman who accompanied him. But his actual response to the news of her presence, his opinion of Malinche's involvement in Cortés's expedition, is not at all clear.

Translation is an imperfect and subjective art famously susceptible to the intrusions of the translator. I am no Nahuatl scholar and my acquaintance with this beautiful language is slight. But my interest in Malinche has made me aware of the curious differences in English-language translations of the Florentine Codex. In the first such work, carried out in the 1970s, word of Malinche's presence among the Spaniards is said to have 'pierced Moctezuma's heart'. In a 1990s' translation, Moctezuma is made to ask indignantly how Malinche could possibly behave as she did, being *'ce cioatl nican titlaca'*, 'a woman among us people here'.

In his own recent work, however, the Nahuatl scholar, James Lockhart, finds no mention of pierced hearts, or fear, or indignation on the part of the Culua-Mexica ruler when he learns of Malinche's existence and her presence among the Spaniards. In Lockhart's careful and precise translation, the passage in question simply says: 'it was told, presented, made known, announced, and reported to Moteucçoma . . . that a woman, one of us people here, came accompanying them as interpreter. Her name was Marina.'

It is interesting in the context of Malinche's role as interpreter, to reflect once more on the protocols for public discourse in Culua-Mexica society. The significance of speech is manifest in the underlying meaning of Moctezuma's title. European history might remember him as an 'emperor', 'ruler', 'king', 'prince', 'lord', or even 'leader', that safer, more generic term. But his own people know him as their *Tlatoani*: 'the Speaker', 'He Who Speaks'. At a deep semantic level this word is not equivalent to those European concepts. Although the *Tlatoani* was an elite warrior and a high priest of their supreme deity, most importantly, he *spoke* for his people.

As far as women were concerned, however, the attitude of Culua-Mexica society seems to have been clear and unequivocal. Women, regardless of their class or status, were explicitly forbidden from speaking out on high matters of religion and state. They had no official voice.

Yet there on the causeway leading into the imperial city, stood Malinche. In front of all who had gathered to watch and listen, she spoke directly to their *Tlatoani*, and he, for the sake of diplomacy and intelligibility, was obliged to converse with her. The sound of her voice, a woman's voice, engaged in such high-level governmental discourse, must have rocked Moctezuma's sensibilities to the core, and those of his people. She may not have been a member of Culua-Mexica society, but her behaviour was unprecedented for a woman.

Did Malinche bow to the powerful weight of Amerindian orthodoxy and avert her eyes as she addressed Moctezuma? Or did she take her cues from the Spaniards who accompanied her? The Florentine Codex does not tell us. Or rather, it does not do so in words. In one of its many illustrations, however, in plate 45 to be precise, Malinche gazes directly into Moctezuma's eyes, while the familiar glyph for speech, a small curling tongue, floats in the air between them. In Moctezuma's terms it would have been unthinkable, an act of desecration, that such a woman, a former slave from beyond the southern reaches of his empire, should stare into his eyes like this.

MALINCHE GAZES INTO MOCTEZUMA'S FACE

(from the Florentine Codex, c. 1550)

The illustration is not a photographic record of what happened that day on the causeway. Like the text of the Florentine Codex it was prepared around thirty-six years after the event. But in depicting Malinche like this it reveals something of the way in which those young Nahuatl scholars remembered her: as an iconoclast, a taboo-breaker, a woman to whom the normal conventions no longer applied.

Knowing as we now do, the ultimate outcome of this swaggering entrance of foreigners into his city, Moctezuma's behaviour seems, at first, both naïve and feckless, especially when set against the apparently steady, inexorable tread of Hernan Cortés toward Tenochtitlan. Why, for example, did Moctezuma welcome the Spaniards when he could have crushed them with one mighty blow months earlier as they made their way up from the coast? Is it true that he mistook Cortés for a returning god, a pale-faced divinity called Quetzalcoatl returning from the east to reclaim his kingdom?

This fabulous, enticing legend haunts the pages of enyclopaedias, of histories, of novels and poems. It has become axiomatic to the story of the Conquest wherever it is told, but it is a tale without substance in the contemporary sources. The most recent translator and editor of Cortés's letters, Anthony Pagden, believes it arose later in the sixteenth century, initially among Franciscan evangelists.

The Franciscans took great care to learn what they could about the old religious beliefs of their new flock throughout the conquered territories of present-day Mexico. They are known to have been particularly attracted to the mythology surrounding the peace-loving deity, Quetzalcoatl, who, according to tradition, had been driven into exile in the east.

Quetzalcoatl was not a significant deity to the Culua-Mexica. Their principal male gods were their own warlike Huitzilopochtli and Tezcatlipoca. Quetzalcoatl's legend had belonged to the first great civilisers of the Valley of Mexico, the Toltec. But with his Christ-like attributes this divinity became an important evangelising tool for the Franciscans, and it could do their cause no harm to have Cortés acquire some of this divinity's mythic qualities. Pagden believes it was they who encouraged the belief that Moctezuma mistook Cortés for a returning Quetzalcoatl.

Three hundred years later, this exotic story was repeated for English-speaking readers by the great nineteenth-century historian, William Prescott. Prescott's famous portrait of a noble savage paralysed by his own arcane superstitions, duped by a cunning Renaissance man, found a permanent and enduring place in the popular imagination. Why? Perhaps because it appeals to Western presumptions about the tragic, passive fatalism of 'the indian', and the natural supremacy of rational European man.

The legend has proved as enduring as the myth of Cortés's single-handed victory over the Culua-Mexica. In reality we do not know what Moctezuma made of the *Caxtillan tlaca,* the Castillian people, in general. We have no faithful Bernal Diaz to report his conversations with his nobles. Moctezuma's motivations, his machinations, his plots and schemes, are buried with him in the rubble of Tenochtitlan.

This much we do know. Moctezuma's name meant 'Courageous Lord', and he was not the last great leader of the Culua-Mexica, as is often assumed. That honour and sorrow would fall to his nephew, Cuauhtemoc, who is still revered as a hero in Mexico. Nor was Moctezuma some effete hereditary monarch in the European fashion, for he had been chosen explicitly for his valour and wisdom. Only a supremely courageous warrior could have led a nation of warriors like the Culua-Mexica.

It was his tragedy, however, to be the first of his people to grapple with these audacious visitors with their diplomatic posturings. If Cortés had been less a talker, more openly a man of war, if he had not had Malinche to speak for him, it is possible Moctezuma might have acted differently from the beginning. He did not, and within six months of their entry into Tenochtitlan, he was dead.

In the beginning he had little reason to fear the presence of the newcomers in his city. Tenochtitlan was an island fortress surrounded on all sides by water. The only way out lay along a series of narrow causeways leading back to the mainland. Its population in November 1519 is estimated to have been around 200 000 people, many of whom were warriors as dedicated to warfare as the ancient Spartans had once been. Everything so far in his nation's short, dynamic history would have told Moctezuma that he and his city were invincible.

For all these reasons Tenochtitlan may well have been, from his perspective, a perfect place to lure and keep the five hundred or so Spaniards who had invited themselves into his world. But they had announced themselves as ambassadors, claiming that they represented a great king far across the sea. He received them accordingly, just as they had received his representatives, peacefully and courteously, on the coast eight months earlier, and throughout their journey through the mountains to Tenochtitlan.

Therefore, after insisting the Tlaxcalan and Huejotzingan allies retreat from the causeway, Moctezuma permitted Cortés and his own men to enter Tenochtitlan as his official guests. He probably believed that beneath his watchful eye, within the formidable confines of his city, they would become his prisoners. And for a while, in fact if not in name, they did.

Despite their bloodless entry, the Conquest of Tenochtitlan was not, in the end, an easy victory. It would take two appalling years of battle and retreat, siege and massacre in a plague-weakened city, before the Culua-Mexica finally succumbed, and for much of that time things went terribly wrong for the Spaniards.

During the first weeks, however, the courtly, diplomatic dialogue begun between Moctezuma and Cortés on the causeway continued through Malinche, while Bernal Diaz roamed the city recording what he saw for posterity.

Diaz admired the elegant palace in which Moctezuma resided and the careful ritual with which four beautiful and 'very clean' young women served his meals. He noted with surprise that the Culua-Mexica ruler took a bath each day, 'and the clothes that he wore one day he did not wear again till three or four days later'. It was a revelation to a sixteenth-century European who had lived in his armour for many months now, and for whom bodily cleanliness was of little importance.

Diaz noted that little hunchbacked dwarfs would often entertain Moctezuma while he dined. And since the spectre of cannibalism was a constant concern to the Spaniards in those early days, he took a somewhat anxious interest in Moctezuma's food. He ate such a variety of meats, however, that Diaz found it impossible to determine whether human flesh was included among his dishes.

Diaz watched as the emperor drank *chocolatl* in golden cups, and inhaled perfumed smoke from long painted and gilded tubes, 'in which they put liquid amber mixed with some herbs which are tobacco'. So it is through Diaz's sharp eyes that we read for the first time about chocolate and tobacco, those universally familiar indulgences today.

In the royal armoury Bernal Diaz saw shields and two-handed swords 'richly adorned with gold and precious stones'. He visited the aviary with its royal eagles and brilliant tropical birds from the southern provinces. Among them were the precious quetzal whose sweeping emerald tail feathers were prized above all else by the Culua-Mexica. He roamed through the palace's exquisite scented gardens and the extraordinary marketplace with its gold and silver merchants, chocolate sellers, slave traders and purveyors of jaguar and ocelot skins.

In the end Bernal Diaz gave up attempting to relate all that he saw, saying that if he tried to do so he would never finish. He continued to observe Moctezuma with interest, especially during his many conversations with Cortés through Malinche. Diaz noticed that the emperor 'in his princely manner' often laughed at these times, and that Cortés too was inclined to laugh. The two men addressed each other in flattering terms, he said, with Cortés calling Moctezuma 'Great Prince' and exclaiming that he did not know how to repay his generosity, while Moctezuma addressed Cortés as 'Lord Malinche' and expressed his delight at the presence of such valiant gentlemen in his kingdom.

Extravagant ingratiating dialogues, but probing too, as each man sought to discover, through the woman who stood between them, whatever he could about his counterpart, without revealing too much about himself. It was a delicate business, and this fragile prelude, this phony game of words in which Malinche was essential, could not and did not last.

Gradually the mood within Tenochtitlan deteriorated, and as it became more and more tense, Malinche, as interpreter, was called upon to undertake increasingly terrifying tasks. She went with Cortés, Diaz and Moctezuma one momentous afternoon to the temple of the city's supreme deity, Huitzilopochtli. She saw the idol itself. She saw the walls and floors caked with blood, and the hearts of that day's sacrificial victims still burning in the temple braziers. 'The stench was worse,' Diaz said 'than that of any slaughter house in Spain.'

Malinche would have been accustomed, conceptually at least, to the practice of ritual sacrifice, but the inner sanctum of such a temple would have been as unfamiliar to her as to the Spaniards. To see what she did that day, and live, made her unique among Meso Americans, and she would have known it. In her world only priests and victims made the long and terrible journey up the hundreds of steps to the temple platform, and only the priests returned.

Nevertheless, when the time came for her to speak for Cortés, she did so. She announced to Moctezuma that the idols he cherished were evil things 'the proper name for which is devils'. She told him that he should erect a cross within the temple instead, 'and a statue of Our Lady', and presumably, as he exploded in rage, she cringed with fear. Diaz says Moctezuma's anger was so terrifying that they turned and fled to the safety of their quarters.

From Moctezuma's perspective the curtain had finally been ripped aside. His anger did not abate, and soon after, we cannot be sure how long, perhaps just a matter of days, the Spaniards decided to protect themselves by taking him hostage. Malinche went with Cortés and a party of his men to his palace, and Diaz tells us it was she who informed him, with great formality, that he must accompany them to their quarters as their prisoner.

When he refused, the Spaniards seem to have panicked. They began to argue among themselves, Diaz said, and one man threatened to draw his dagger and murder Moctezuma there and then. In the midst of this menacing chaos of voices, Moctezuma turned to Malinche and asked her to tell him what they were saying. This was the only instance we know of in which Moctezuma spoke to her directly rather than as a spokeswoman for Cortés. Diaz says she advised the Culua-Mexica leader that he should go with them immediately. 'I know they will treat you very honourably as the great prince you are . . . but if you stay here you will be a dead man.'

Perhaps she said more than this. Diaz would not have known exactly what she said. Possibly her advice included warnings about the fate of his wives, his children, his entire family. Malinche's feelings as she performed this unthinkable act of advising the *Tlatoani* of the Culua-Mexica that he was now a prisoner can only be imagined. But if she trembled or faltered at what she was doing, Bernal Diaz did not remark on it.

✣

Little is known about Moctezuma's imprisonment in the Spaniards' quarters, but Diaz assures us he was treated with the respect due to such a distinguished prisoner of war. He also tells us that during that time Moctezuma became attached to a young Spanish page called Juan de Orteguilla who spoke Nahuatl quite well. Malinche, it seems, had been tutoring him.

Moctezuma asked his young attendant many questions about this land called Spain from where his captors said they had come, and no doubt Orteguilla was able to furnish the Spaniards with whatever information he obtained from their illustrious captive.

Meanwhile Diaz found his own use for the page's linguistic skills. 'I talked to Orteguilla,' he said, 'and asked him to beg Moctezuma kindly to give me a pretty Indian girl.' His request, it seems, was granted, for to his joy Moctezuma gave him one of his own concubines. We never hear a word about this young woman. She was just another casualty of war, like Malinche herself. Diaz says only that she was given the name Doña Francisca, 'and her bearing showed her distinction'.

Moctezuma died six months later in mysterious circumstances. Cortés and Diaz always claimed the ruler's own people had killed him, but the Culua-Mexica believed, probably correctly, that the

Spaniards had secretly murdered him, when it became apparent
that their attempt to rule through him had failed. For by now the
Spaniards themselves were virtual prisoners in their quarters, and
outside the city streets were in uproar.

Shortly after Moctezuma's death, eight months after their
entry into Tenochtitlan, the Spaniards attempted to escape
unnoticed but, the story goes, an old woman saw them, raised
the alarm, and they fled in panic and disarray.

In the darkness of night, with the city's finest warriors on their
heels, the Spaniards were driven away in a humiliating and
desperate retreat. Many drowned in the waters of Lake Texcoco,
weighed down by their heavy armour. Others were captured,
dragged to the temple platforms and sacrificed.

It was the night of 30 June 1520, a night the Spaniards called
La Noche Triste, the Sorrowful Night. Sorrowful for them,
triumphant for the people of Tenochtitlan. Bernal Diaz recalled
later that amid the chaos of retreat Malinche was found
miraculously alive at one of the bridges on the principal
causeway. A slight dark figure, dressed simply in *huipil* and
sandals, perhaps with a shawl about her head, she must have
moved swiftly along the shadows of the causeway, camouflaging
herself in a way the Spaniards could not hope to do.

But Tenochtitlan's triumph was tragically short lived. We
know now that Cortés's most implacable, most indomitable ally
in the eventual Conquest was not human, but pathogenic, and
that by the time the Spaniards fled, smallpox had already entered
the city. Among the first of the epidemic's many thousands of
victims was Moctezuma's successor, Cuitlahuac. It was at this

point that his nephew, Cuauhtemoc, a young man probably no more than twenty-two, became the last leader of the Culua-Mexica.

While European disease ravaged Tenochtitlan, Cortés's men, who like most adult Spaniards were immune to smallpox, found sanctuary with their Tlaxcalan allies in the mountains beyond the city. They felled trees and constructed a fleet of brigantines and in May 1521, almost a year after their retreat from the city, launched their ships for the final terrible battle for Tenochtitlan.

As long as Malinche's voice was required in the frontline beside Cortés, she is visible to us through the eyes and ears of Bernal Diaz who recorded what he saw and heard. But when the talking stops and the fighting begins, she appears only rarely, presumably because Diaz was too occupied with the business of killing to take note of her movements.

But others did. Sometime during the mid-nineteenth century a collection of Nahuatl poems, believed to have been composed shortly after the Conquest, came to light. They had been written, like the Florentine Codex, in the Roman script, and in them we glimpse Malinche at the launch of the brigantines.

Tonaye malintzin, 'Mother Malintzin', she is called, as she shouts encouragement to a Tlaxcalan warrior. 'Yellow Beak, my lookout!' she cries. 'You've arrived in Acachinanco! Be strong! Hail!' In another of these poems, the tragic 'Water Pouring Song', she appears as *Malia teuccihuatl*, 'Lady Malia'. 'O Mexicans,' she cries, 'your water jars go here! Let all the lords come carrying!'

There is a poignant metaphorical link, the translator tells us, between the pouring of water and the pouring of Culua-Mexica blood. With Malinche as the agent of destruction.

There are other suggestions of her active participation in the combat. The Tlaxcalan history of the Conquest, the *Lienzo de Tlaxcala*, in which she is always an heroic figure, depicts her aboard one of the brigantines, carrying a shield as the battle for Tenochtitlan rages.

An illustration in the Florentine Codex shows her on the roof of one of Tenochtitlan's palaces. While Cortés watches, she summons the Culua-Mexica nobles and warriors below to bring water and food for the Spaniards. 'Mexicans, come here!' she cries. 'The

MALINCHE WITH SHIELD

(from Lienzo de Tlaxcala, c. 1550)

Spaniards have tired themselves. Bring them food, fresh water, and all that is needed. For they have wearied themselves, they are exhausted.'

The desperate, dying city surrendered after three months of siege on 13 August 1521. Or, according to the Florentine Codex: 'And when the shield was laid down, when we gave way, it was the year count Three House and the day count One Serpent.'

Bernal Diaz said there was a great storm that night, of the frightening capricious sort that still engulfs Mexico City in summer. It rained and thundered and lightning flashed. Throughout the siege the clamour of kettledrums and flutes and trumpets on the temple platforms never ceased, nor the cries of the war leaders directing and encouraging their warriors, calling to the women and children gathering stones in the streets and shaping them for their slings. Afterwards a terrible quiet fell over what remained of the city 'as if all the bells in the belfry had been ringing and then suddenly stopped'.

The silence of death descended on Tenochtitlan. Men, women and children 'so thin, sallow, dirty and stinking that it was pitiful to see them' streamed out of the city along the causeways piled with the dead. In the remaining houses survivors too ill and emaciated to move, lay dying among the rotting corpses of their families. 'Their excretions,' Diaz observed, 'were the sort of filth that thin swine pass which have been fed on nothing but grass.' And the Culua-Mexica's enemies from across the mountains, the Tlaxcalans and Huejotzingans who had come arrayed for war, who had fought and hacked and killed alongside the Spaniards, rejoiced at their annihilation.

According to the Florentine Codex, at the moment of formal surrender Malinche positioned herself beside Cortés and translated for the Culua-Mexica leader, Cuauhtemoc, as he declared that he could do no more for his city or his people. He implored Cortés to take his dagger and kill him immediately so that he might die an honourable death. His wish was not granted; he was condemned to live another four years as the Spaniards' hostage, to die far from home in the land of the Maya.

Throughout the business of surrender, the searching for gold, the sharing out of the spoils, the evacuation of the fallen city, we glimpse Malinche again from time to time in her role as interpreter, but when all is settled she gradually fades from view, and the next three years of her life are lived behind the walls of Cortés's house, well out of reach of chroniclers such as Bernal Diaz.

We know, however, that in May or June the following year she gave birth to her son, Martin, Cortés's first acknowledged child.

III

aftermath

I replied that if he wished to know the truth
he had only to ask the interpreter with whom
he was speaking, Marina, whom I have
always had with me.

HERNAN CORTÉS, 3 SEPTEMBER 1526

Letters from Mexico

The Place of the Coyote

I was living now not far from the statue of Moctezuma's valiant nephew, Cuauhtemoc. He stands high above the city's most beautiful avenue, gazing west toward the Bosque de Chapultepec. Cuauhtemoc's name is as venerated among Mexicans as Moctezuma's is despised, and with the election only a month away supporters of the various political parties would gather beneath this tragic youth's figure to claim him as their patron.

On the verandah outside the kitchen a wooden box of melons was ripening in the sun, and in the small garden lizards and hummingbirds flourished. The domesticity of life here calmed and restored me, and I realised how dislocated I had felt in the south, and so visible, with my strange clothes and curious accent. The tropical heat had sapped my strength but back in this mountain city the summer mornings were cool, and I could pass in the street unnoticed, anonymous among the twenty million other residents.

On the southern side of the city is a fashionable suburb called Coyoacan that was once a separate town on the shores of Lake

Texcoco. Coyoacan's name means 'the place of the coyote' in Nahuatl, but it is the haunt of students, artists and intellectuals now, and more a place of their beloved icons than of coyotes. Diego Rivera and Frida Kahlo lived and worked in Coyoacan, and it was in Coyoacan too, that the exiled Leon Trotsky met his infamous death at the hands of an assassin with an ice-pick. The houses of all three are considered sacred shrines.

In Coyoacan there is another house, however, far older but less celebrated. It was constructed soon after the fall of Tenochtitlan, on the site of a Culua-Mexica palace, and if the stories about it are true, Malinche was among its first residents. Filomena Alvarado had warned me about its owner: 'She is a member of the Coyoacan bourgeoisie,' she told me. 'She will have no sympathy for Malinche.' I wanted to hear for myself what this woman thought about Malinche. I didn't wish to invade her privacy but I sent her a letter.

'As an outsider,' I wrote, 'I find it puzzling and paradoxical that in Mexico today Malinche should be denounced for her part in the Conquest. I wonder what you think about her? Do you believe in her supposed treachery? Were her actions any different from those of the men of Tlaxcala and Huejotzingo? As the custodian of what was once Malinche's house you are in a unique position, and I would value your opinion.' I received no reply. Perhaps the letter did not reach her. Perhaps she found it obnoxious, or the subject of Malinche too odious or too tiresome to consider.

I went to Coyoacan anyway, with Filomena, and together we contemplated the house on Calle Higuera. Little is known of

Malinche's life in this building, but we know that she was not the only woman within its walls. It was Cortés's official household, and in the manner of a great medieval lord he had taken Moctezuma's daughters beneath his wing as their protector. He claimed he did this in accordance with Moctezuma's last wishes, but no one knew for certain. In any case, who was in a position to stop him?

This was a common practice in the wars of conquest in the Americas. Twelve years later the conqueror of Peru, Cortés's kinsman, Francisco Pizarro, would similarly declare himself the official protector of the Inca Atahualpa's children. There was more to this custom, of course, than simple charity or soldiers' honour. These noble offspring lived in comfort but under virtual house arrest. They were, in reality, hostages for peace.

So in the aftermath of the fall of Tenochtitlan, Moctezuma's daughters lived in Cortés's household, bringing him prestige, legitimacy and security. They were essential to him as he sought to rule a restive colony of bitter, vanquished Culua-Mexica survivors and disgruntled conquistadors who felt that Cortés had cheated them in the distribution of the booty of conquest.

The highest ranking of these young noblewomen was Doña Isabel, known before the Conquest as Tecuichpotzin. A year earlier, at the height of the war in Tenochtitlan, she had been married to her cousin, Cuauhtemoc, for precisely the same reason that Cortés had declared himself her protector. Because in their hour of crisis the Culua-Mexica nobility required the authority, the sense of continuity she carried with her, as Moctezuma's only surviving legitimate daughter.

It was a formal marriage, but possibly never consummated since she was only twelve years old at the time. At the moment of the Culula-Mexica surrender she had been forcibly separated from Cuauhtemoc, and she was never permitted to live with him again. With Doña Isabel in the house in Coyoacan were her three half-sisters. Their Nahuatl names are lost to us, but by then they were called Doña Maria, Doña Ana and, just to complicate matters, Doña Marina. So now there were two Doña Marinas in Cortés's life.

Of all the souls beneath his roof, these four young noble-women, especially Doña Isabel, were the most important. Malinche, on the other hand, had outlived her usefulness for the moment. She had no official role to play, and her status is unclear. Unlike Moctezuma's daughters she had no great lineage to protect her. She depended for her welfare entirely on Cortés's gratitude, a far less reliable safeguard. A romantic interpretion of her story would suggest that, as his mistress, she might have enjoyed his natural devotion, but there is no evidence to suggest that this was so.

The domestic sphere of women in the past is a landscape notoriously difficult to chart. Occasionally, if we are lucky, they leave diaries or letters or even household account books from which we may piece together something of their hidden world. Malinche left no such treasures. It is possible, however, to retrieve some details of life within this household and to infer from them what Malinche's place may have been in Cortés's scheme of things. The information comes from a surprising source and the story it tells us is not encouraging.

In 1529 Cortés's life became the focus of official scrutiny, when the Spanish Crown established a judicial enquiry called a *Residencia*, to investigate his governance of what was now called New Spain. This vast new province stretched from Guatemala in the south as far as California in the north, for once Tenochtitlan had been secured the wars of conquest had continued as wave after wave of adventurer arrived on Mexican shores. As the indigenous peoples of other continents like Africa and Australia would one day learn to their great sorrow, the momentum of European invasion, once unleashed, was impossible to stop.

Cortés's *Residencia* was the first such enquiry to be held in New Spain, and it was a long and painstaking affair conducted with the careful bureaucratic tenacity for which sixteenth-century Spain was renowned. A formidable retinue of judges arrived from Spain, and a legion of witnesses was called to testify before them. They were questioned under oath about every conceivable aspect of Cortés's conduct, including, as it happens, his relations with the women beneath his roof.

The witnesses were asked if they had heard that Cortés had lived carnally with the daughters of Moctezuma, and with a woman called Mariana, 'a woman of this land', and with a daughter of hers. Who is this 'Mariana'? She is 'a woman of this land' but not, apparently, one of Moctezuma's daughters. As 'Mariana' was a frequent variation of the name Marina, this must be a reference to Malinche, or Marina, as the Spaniards always called her.

It is in the phrasing of this interrogatory that we hear the first whisper of a daughter who may have come with her from

Potonchan. Several of the witnesses responded, however, that the girl in question was not Malinche's daughter but her niece. Some even ventured a name for her, Catalina. If what they say is true, this young girl might have been with Malinche all this time, in her care, but unmentioned, unnoticed until now. For in the context of what they had all been through, who would notice such a child?

The shipwrecked priest and former interpreter, Geronimo de Aguilar, came forward to testify against his old commander. He said that the daughters of various lords lived in the house at Coyoacan, and that Cortés had sexual relations with all of them, despite the fact that they were related to each other. Consanguinity among Cortés's mistresses often seems to have concerned Aguilar and the other witnesses more than any other aspect of their former commander's sexual conduct.

But Aguilar makes it quite clear in his accusation against Cortés that he is referring to Malinche, or 'Marina the interpreter' as he calls her. He told the tribunal that Cortés knew Marina the interpreter carnally, '*se echo carnalmente con Marina*', and she had borne a son to him.

That Cortés had a passion for women seems certain, but like any powerful man in any time he had numerous enemies and a host of willing accusers, especially among his former comrades in arms. They felt he had never repaid them, as he had promised he would, for their actions in the Conquest of Tenochtitlan. Bernal Diaz describes, for example, the graffiti scrawled across Cortés's wall in Coyoacan. 'Not conquerors, but conquered by Cortés' it read, and Cortés, Diaz records, responded with his own mocking slogan: 'White walls, paper of fools.'

In such a bitter ambience it is possible that many of these testimonies were shaped and exaggerated by enmity. But if even a little of what these voices tell us is correct, it suggests that the household at Coyoacan was never a haven of conjugal bliss for Malinche, or any of the other women who lived there.

Sometime early in 1522, Malinche's son, Martin Cortés, was born. We know nothing of her confinement. Was it difficult? Was she alone, or assisted by other women, and if so, by whom? Perhaps the mysterious girl, her daughter or niece, was with her. Perhaps a professional midwife came forward from among the Culua-Mexica survivors of Tenochtitlan, or even one of the Spanish women who had survived the conquest with Malinche.

Cortés later took great pains to have his *mestizo* son legitimised by papal decree and made a knight of the Order of Santiago, and when Cortés died he left this child a handsome inheritance. But Martin's birth occurred at an awkward moment for, about the time he was born, a ship arrived on the coast of Mexico with Cortés's wife on board, the wife he had left behind in Cuba.

Bernal Diaz was among the party sent to escort her inland to meet her husband, and he later remarked that it was obvious Cortés was far from pleased to see her. This unfortunate woman's time in the house in Coyoacan was both unhappy and brief. She died there in suspicious circumstances, and the shadow of her death was to haunt Cortés for the remainder of his life.

Her name was Catalina Juarez de Marcaida, and by the time the *Residencia* tribunal began its hearings in 1529, she had been dead for seven years and Cortés was far away in Spain. But the question of her death was raised at the inquest, and several of her serving women gave evidence implicating Cortés in her sudden and mysterious demise.

The witnesses told the *Residencia* judges that it had happened in the early hours of All Saints' Day, in November 1522. They said that Cortés had called them to the bedchamber he shared with Catalina and told them she was dead. Some of them claimed to have seen her body, and to have noted bruising and a broken bead necklace around her neck. Their testimony and the fact that Cortés had summoned carpenters and placed his wife's body in a closed coffin without allowing time for the usual vigil to be observed, suggested to many of his contemporaries that he had murdered her.

There was further circumstantial evidence. Catalina's maid, a woman called Ana Rodriguez, testified that her mistress had been deeply distressed by the harem-like atmosphere she encountered in the house at Coyoacan. Another woman, Maria Hernandez, testified that Catalina had told her she was frightened of her husband, saying he had beaten her at times.

Cortés was never tried for his wife's murder. Catalina's mother brought a criminal suit against him and pursued him through the courts for years to come, but in the end she abandoned her action, presumably because she felt she could achieve nothing.

All this occurred within the space of just a few years, inside the walls of that graceful old house in Coyoacan. A tragic death, a controversy never resolved, a man of dissolute reputation with Moctezuma's daughters in his custody, along with Malinche and the young girl who was reputed to have been with her. It can hardly be described as a setting of connubial bliss for Malinche and Cortés, and in any case her residence there came to an end in 1524.

In October that year, she left the house in Coyoacan, and as far as we know she never returned to it. Her interpreting skills were required once more, and she departed on her final journey with Cortés. This time they would travel far to the south, to the Gulf of Honduras in pursuit of a renegade Spanish expedition. Inspired, no doubt, by his own maverick spirit, the rebels had formed a breakaway colony of their own.

Final Journey

'I departed from this great city,' Cortés wrote, 'with a few horsemen, and foot soldiers, men of my own household and my friends and relatives . . . likewise I took with me all the principal natives of this land.'

It was 12 October 1524, and the expedition was heading for what is now Honduras in the realm of the Maya. Once more Malinche would be required to interpret for Cortés. Cuauhtemoc of Tenochtitlan travelled with the expedition, for he was still Cortés's hostage, but Geronimo de Aguilar was left behind in the fallen city. He seems to have already been counted among Cortés's enemies. In any case, Malinche must by now have been fluent in Spanish, so his presence was unnecessary.

The expedition would last two years, and prove a personal and political disaster for Cortés. It was also a momentous journey for Malinche, for just a few weeks after their departure from Tenochtitlan, somewhere on that well-travelled road to the gulf coast, she was married to a Spaniard called Juan Xaramillo de Salvatierra. Her wedding is believed to have taken place on 20 October, somewhere in the vicinity of the present city of Orizaba, beneath the great volcanic peak of the same name.

The precise location of Malinche's marriage is uncertain, but during the 1930s the Mexican historian Gustavo Rodriguez visited the village of Huilopan, just south of Orizaba, and claimed to have found an inscription there, in the keystone of its very old church. Rodriguez thought he could just make out a date, 1524, and the words 'Fr. Juan', which he took to be a reference to Juan de Tecto, the learned theologian from the Sorbonne and former confessor to King Charles of Spain who had conducted Malinche's wedding ceremony.

Malinche's marriage to Juan Xaramillo de Salvatierra erupts into her story without warning and we know nothing of what precipitated it. Had there been some kind of open courtship, or a dalliance behind Cortés's back? That careful observer, Bernal Diaz, had not yet joined the expedition, and cannot give us his version of events. After the fall of Tenochtitlan, he had settled on the gulf coast of the Isthmus of Tehuantepec. But Cortés's first biographer, Francisco López de Gómara, later claimed that Juan Xaramillo had been drunk during the ceremony. Gómara was not present either, but as Cortés's chaplain it is possible he heard this story from Cortés's own lips.

Bernal Diaz refused to believe it. He was always Malinche's champion, and he had no time for Gómara or his biography. He said he knew a man called Aranda, 'a settler in Tabasco', who was present at the wedding, 'and this man told me about the marriage (not in the way the historian Gómara relates it)'. In spite of Diaz's well-meant protestations, however, the story of the bridegroom's drunkenness casts a dubious shadow over this marriage.

We know that Juan Xaramillo was one of Cortés's most trusted officers and that he had captained one of the brigantines during the siege of Tenochtitlan. Like Cortés and so many of the early conquistadors he hailed from the southern Spanish province of Extremadura. He later testified in a statement of his duties to the Crown that he was the son of Don Alonso Xaramillo and Doña Mencia de Matos.

None of this throws any light on Malinche's marriage to this man, and Gómara's sordid whisper suggests at least two unhappy possibilities: that the wedding was a soldierly prank played on an inebriated Xaramillo, or that Cortés forced him to marry her as revenge for some kind of indiscretion between them.

It is also possible that the entire affair revolved around property. Cortés had recently promulgated a law requiring every bachelor to marry, and every married Spaniard to send to Cuba, or to Spain, for his wife. Non-compliance would be punished by forfeiture of any land holdings, and since Juan Xaramillo was the holder of a very rich estate to the north of Tenochtitlan, he would have needed a wife to secure his possessions.

Almost twenty years later several old conquistadors testified in a law suit relating to Xaramillo's will that on Malinche's wedding day Cortés gave her Olutla and Texixtepec, those Isthmus villages which had once been subject to Jaltipan. If this is true then it is possible Xaramillo believed that marriage to Malinche would increase his wealth. Yet there is no official record of such a gift, and by 1550 the two villages in question are noted in the colonial records as belonging to another conquistador, Luis Marin. What of that melancholy story the iguana seller had told me in Jaltipan? That the only land Cortés had given Malinche was the worthless island of Tacamichapa.

Why not consider love as a motivation for Malinche's marriage to Xaramillo? Because although informal marriages between conquistadors and Amerindian women were already commonplace, formal marriages were not. If Juan Xaramillo were anywhere near as ambitious as his peers, it is unlikely he would have willingly settled down with one of his commander's cast-off mistresses.

Malinche may have been born into the provincial nobility, but Xaramillo would have been aiming for a wife of serious rank and means. One of Moctezuma's daughters or nieces, for example, whose position and entitlements to land had been recognised by the Spanish Crown. Or a scion, even slightly removed, of the Spanish aristocracy.

As always with these fragments of Malinche's life there are no clear answers, just a handful of stories, an abundance of rumours, handed down through the centuries. You listen, you weigh the possibilities, and in interpreting what you hear, you try to steer a path between romance and cynicism, accepting that you will never know for certain what went on behind the shield of her marriage to Juan Xaramillo.

In December the expedition arrived near the present-day port of Coatzocoalcos, where Bernal Diaz joined it. So Malinche had come full circle; she had returned to the Isthmus of Tehuantepec, but it was no longer independent territory for the Isthmus too had finally fallen to the Spaniards.

While they were stationed in Coatzocoalcos, Cortés sent messengers throughout the province to summon all its native leaders to his presence 'in order to make them a speech about our holy religion'. Bernal Diaz writes that among those who arrived were Malinche's mother, Marta, and her half-brother, Lázaro. This then is the moment of the family's emotional and short-lived reunion.

Diaz says that Marta and Lázaro wept in fear as they came forward to meet Malinche, believing she had returned to punish them for the way they had treated her some some fourteen years earlier. But she did not castigate them. Instead, in front of all those assembled, she consoled them, giving them some jewels and fine cloth and urging them to return in peace to their town. Bernal Diaz wrote: 'It was easy enough to see that she was the daughter from the strong likeness she bore to her mother.'

Diaz said Malinche made a fine speech, telling her mother and brother that God had been gracious in freeing her from the worship of idols and making her a Christian, in letting her bear a son to her lord and master, Cortés, and in marrying her to a gentleman like Juan Xaramillo. She assured them that she would rather serve her husband and Cortés than be ruler of all the provinces in New Spain.

This moving account is the only one we have of the tearful meeting at Coatzocoalcos. Diaz quotes Malinche's words as if verbatim, but we cannot be certain how well he understood what she was saying, for he was not yet, as far as we can tell, a Nahuatl speaker. It is possible he inferred what she said from her intonations and her gestures as she calmed her weeping relatives. Or that after she made her speech in Nahuatl, she gave it a second time in Spanish for the edification of her Spanish companions.

However it was played out, this episode made a profound impression on Bernal Diaz, and he had no doubts about what he saw and heard that day in Coatzocoalcos. He relays Malinche's words with the exemplary ring of a parable, and her apparent act of forgiveness moved him to compare her to Joseph in the Book of Genesis when he forgave his brothers for selling him into slavery.

So Malinche was reunited with her family. Perhaps she could have returned to them at this point, but she did not. Like the shipwrecked Spaniard Gonzalo Guerrero, still living somewhere in the south with his Mayan wife and children, she appears to have cast her lot with her adoptive people.

Malinche returned to the Isthmus, but she never saw the city of Potonchan again, where she had lived among the Maya, or the old trade enclave of Xicalango, where she had been sold into slavery. For after Coatzocoalcos the expedition turned inland and began to negotiate the treacherous marshes and quicksands to its south, constructing makeshift bridges as they went, building rafts and commandeering canoes from local villagers.

Somewhere near the present-day city of Villa Hermosa, they crossed the Grijalva River, then the Usumacinta. They struggled on into the Mayan province of Acalan, through an enormous swamp which Cortés called 'the most terrible thing that man ever saw'. There, on the banks of the Candelaria, another great brown river flowing in from Guatemala, the Spaniards executed Cuauhtemoc and the other Culua-Mexica noblemen they had dragged with them on this hideous journey. Bernal Diaz tells us candidly that the murder of Cuauhtemoc caused dismay and unrest among the Spaniards. Many of them complained openly, he says, that Cortés was wrong to execute him.

So why did Cortés take this brutal and controversial step? Did he act in panic because he feared he was losing his grip over the expedition? Perhaps he executed Cuauhtemoc as a show trial, in order to terrorise the people of Acalan and to impress his own men with his authority. In his next letter to the King of Spain he justified his actions by describing Cuauhtemoc as a dangerous man, too dangerous to be permitted to live: 'A turbulent person,' he called him, 'and the cause of all insecurity and revolt in this country.'

In 1933, while the scholar France Scholes was reading in the Archivo General de Indias in Seville, he discovered a rare Mayan text written sometime late in the sixteenth century in the Roman script and by an unknown hand. This precious document records the tragic, shameful episode of Cuauhtemoc's execution. It tells us that Malinche was with the Culua-Mexica leader and prayed for him in Nahuatl at the moment of his death.

Bernal Diaz said Cuauhtemoc made an anguished speech through Malinche, and she appeared to translate his words without diminishing in any way the strength of the accusations they contained. Cuauhtemoc denounced Cortés for dragging him all that way just to murder him, she said. He asked why

Cortés could not have killed him honourably, four years earlier, at the fall of Tenochtitlan, as he had wished.

Cuauhtemoc was executed on 28 February, the eve of Ash Wednesday, 1525. The method of his execution has never been clear. Some accounts claim he was decapitated, others that he was hanged. However it was done, his body was hung from a tree in Acalan and left to rot like a criminal's, far from his home and his people.

Bernal Diaz recalled later that after Cuauhtemoc's death Cortés began drinking heavily, even before breakfast, 'something he never used to do in the earlier wars'. His journey through the swamps of the Isthmus and the steaming jungles of what is now Guatemala had been nothing like his triumphant entrance into Tenochtitlan, with the pounding of hooves, the ringing of bridle bells, with the standard 'rising like a warrior'.

On this second expedition Cortés had seen his men drown in quicksand, die horribly of tropical fevers and fight like dogs over food. By the time he reached the ancient town of Tayasal on the shores of Lake Peten, close to where the beautiful ruined temples of Tikal still soar above the rainforest, he was so broken in health and morale that he received a puzzled reception from the Itza Mayan lord, who had no idea who this pitiable stranger was, with his bedraggled expedition.

As Malinche delivered her customary speech on Cortés's behalf, the lord of Tayasal seemed to recognise certain features of the story she told of the conquest of the Culua-Mexica, of a great king across the eastern sea, of the one true cross. When she had finished speaking, the Mayan leader recalled that a party of merchants from Potonchan had passed this way some years earlier, and told him of a great captain who had entered their land and defeated them in battle. He wondered, rather hesitantly, whether Cortés could possibly be that man.

It was the first time in many years that Cortés had been obliged to explain and verify his greatness. 'I replied,' he wrote later, 'that if he wished to learn the truth he had only to ask the interpreter with whom he was speaking, Marina, whom I have always had with me.' And speaking in the Mayan tongue she had acquired as a slave, Malinche assured the lord of Tayasal that Cortés was indeed the famous warrior who had conquered Potonchan seven years earlier.

Cortés had turned to her for the support and validation that she alone, who had been through everything with him, could give. It is the first and only time in his famous letters that he refers to her by name. It is also her final bow on the stage of history.

The expedition reached the Gulf of Honduras some weeks later, only to find that most of the Spanish insurrectionists they had come so far to apprehend had died the previous year. Some had perished from tropical fevers, others had been killed in a series of violent disputes. Cortés managed to purchase three caravels from the survivors of the rebel colony and with the remnants of his own depleted expedition, he sailed back around the stretch of coast where he had rescued Geronimo de Aguilar seven years earlier.

The return voyage was as disastrous as the long and terrible overland journey had been. Somewhere in that narrow stretch of water that lies between Cuba and the northern tip of the Yucatan Peninsula, the small fleet was engulfed by a furious tropical storm. One of the caravels was lost with all on board, including the learned Juan de Tecto, the priest at Malinche's marriage to Juan Xaramillo. He drowned, leaving unfinished the catechism he had begun writing in Nahuatl.

As for Cortés, when he finally struggled ashore at Veracruz in May 1526, Bernal Diaz writes that at first no one recognised him, for he was so changed: 'During the wars of New Spain, he [Cortés] was lean and with little belly, but after our return from Hibueras [Honduras] he was much more corpulent with a great belly, and I also noticed that the beard which was black before had become whitened.'

Malinche, however, with her extraordinary powers of endurance, had survived yet again, and sometime during that tempestuous voyage back to Veracruz had given birth to a baby girl she called Maria, her only child by Juan Xaramillo. Malinche's movements after this are unknown. Her public life as Cortés's guide and interpreter was over.

Archives

I went back to the house on the Plaza de Santo Domingo, where Malinche is believed to have spent her final years after she returned from Honduras. The grade four teacher was sitting at her table preparing her classes for the next day.

'You've returned!' she exclaimed, pulling up a chair for me.

'Yes,' I said, 'it was a long journey.'

'And the Isthmus?'

'It was beautiful in its own way. I saw the gigantic stone heads the Olmec left behind them and their little jaguar figures, but not the ruins of San Lorenzo, even though I passed very close to them. The heat was intense down there. I found that difficult.'

'Did you see any signs of Malinche?'

'I saw signs, yes. I saw a garden named after her and a little river. I saw the volcano in Tlaxcala and a painting in a church. I talked to people. I gained a stronger sense of her life, her journeys, the enormous distances she travelled.'

'What will you do now?' the teacher asked me.

'I haven't got much longer in Mexico,' I told her. 'I want to spend some time in the various archives, just to see, you know, if I can find some clue about how she ended her days.'

'Is there anything we can do to help you, here in the school?'

'Well, I like to be here, to visit like this,' I said. 'It means a great deal to me, just knowing that Malinche may once have lived within these walls.'

❧

Does any city preserve its ancestry with as much fervour as Mexico City? It seems that every time work begins anywhere in the old quarter, whether for an extension to the metro, or to replace faulty sewage pipes, another fragment, another layer of the Amerindian past is revealed. So streets and footpaths are redirected, construction plans are altered, while years of patient disclosure begin in the excavation sites.

Mexico's post-Conquest past is preserved with just as much reverence in the Archivo General de la Nacion. The Archivo is set back from the road, surrounded by an arbour of trees. It is an enormous stone building, solid and imposing, with crennellated towers at each corner: a former prison. Guards checked my identification at the front door and ensured that I registered my name, the date and time of my arrival. They told me I could take nothing with me except a notebook and pen, but they allowed me my Spanish dictionary when I explained how much I needed it.

Inside, at the top of the stairs, beneath a magnificent dome, a young librarian beckoned me to a chair at the desk beside her.

She asked what my field of study was and I began, rather hesitantly at first, to explain my interest in Malinche. In Mexico I often hesitated like this, fearing what? Ridicule? Or perhaps because Malinche is such an essential and controversial element in Mexico's national mythology, that they would be offended by my interest in her.

The librarian looked up from the researcher's card she was preparing for me.

'It's curious,' she said putting down her pen, 'but I have never really thought much about her. To us, she is not so much a real woman. She is more an abstraction, an idea, a symbol — an injurious symbol in many ways, at least for we Mexican women.'

'Yes,' I said. 'I have come to that conclusion too.'

'But if you have come here to the Archivo,' she continued, 'does this mean you are more concerned with her life than with her symbolism?'

'No,' I replied, 'I'm interested in both, in the ways the threads run together. Or the ways they diverge.'

She nodded. 'You wish to compare the myth with the reality?'

'Yes,' I replied. 'The woman and what was made of her. Perhaps that is the most important part of all.'

I told the librarian I had come to the Archivo because I was curious about how and when Malinche might have died.

'I'm afraid there will be no easy way for you to ascertain this,' she said. 'Deaths were not registered in the City of Mexico until 1671, marriages a century earlier, baptisms from 1537.' She had completed my researcher's card and she handed it to me across the desk.

'If you find anything it will probably be by accident, in some passing reference, or a slip of the tongue. Archival research is like hunting for *una aguja en un pajar*,' she said.

'Yes,' I nodded, 'a needle in a haystack.'

'I wish you luck,' she said, 'and courage.'

There is a letter in the Archivo General, written in 1551 by a certain Don Martin Cortés, alluding to a street in which 'doña Marina lives at present'. This reference has suggested to many historians that the Don Martin Cortés who wrote this letter was Malinche's son, and that Malinche was still alive in 1551. It is an understandable assumption given the coincidence of these two familiar names. However, the author of this letter was not Malinche's child Martin; he was Martin's half-brother, born in 1531 to Hernan Cortés and his second wife, Juana de Zuñiga. As Cortés's first legitimate son he too had been named for his paternal grandfather. By the time the younger Don Martin wrote this letter in 1551, his father had been dead for four years and he had inherited the title the Spanish Crown had bestowed on his father. He had become the second Marquis of the Valley of Oaxaca.

As for the Doña Marina of this letter, she was not Malinche. She was the Spanish-born, wealthy and attractive widow of the Royal Treasurer, and there were rumours in New Spain that she was having an affair with the younger Don Martin Cortés, who wrote this letter. Her full name was Marina Gutierrez Flores de la Caballeria, an elaborate designation even by Spanish standards.

If it seems absurd that Cortés should have given the same name to two children, his family tree shows that he did this constantly. His four legitimate children were called Martin, Luis, Catalina and Maria, and so were his four illegitimate offspring, like matching pairs, in and out of wedlock. But 'Catalina' was especially precious to Cortés because it had been his own mother's name. Therefore, when his first legitimate daughter called Catalina died in infancy, he used the name once more, for his second legitimate daughter.

By the time I walked down the polished corridors of the Archivo General in Mexico City, I knew all this. But somewhere in the depths of the Archivo, I hoped it might be possible to determine what had happened to Malinche after she returned from Honduras.

You wouldn't think a piece of written testimony scrawled on a yellowed sheet of parchment could be so electrifying. You ask yourself who else has touched it, who else has read it, since it was signed and sealed and stored away so long ago.

You wouldn't think those commonplace referents such as 'mother', or 'mother-in-law', or 'grandmother', could mean so much. But there is a life-giving force in the familiarity of these words, especially where a woman like Malinche is concerned. It is the sense they give, no matter how elusive, of the flesh and blood woman behind the myth, of someone's mother, someone's wife.

I sat reading from two heavy volumes of Inquisition documents on the long wooden table before me. Anyone who knows modern Spanish can decipher its sixteenth-century antecedent with little difficulty, in printed form at least, for it has altered much less than English in the past five hundred years. But the stiff parchments in front of me that morning were covered in a terrifying, spidery scrawl. Fascinating but unintelligible, they might just as well have been written in Arabic or Hebrew.

I made out a word, then another, as little by little I adjusted to the individual handwriting of the scribes who had penned all those testimonies so long ago. I began to recognise their idiosyncrasies, the small shifts and changes in orthography, the transposition of certain letters.

In the top right-hand corner of the first page one simple phrase was immediately legible, because I was anticipating it. '*Limpieza de sangre*', it announced, literally 'cleanliness of blood'. A simple term, a sinister concept. I thought of Bosnia, of Rwanda, of Nazi Germany. Will we never be free of its hideous resonance? It explained why the Inquisition was investigating the geneology of Don Manuel Villegas and his wife, Doña Margarita de Peralta. To ensure that neither of them had a Jew or a Moor in their ancestry.

I found the testimony I was looking for. It had been sworn by Juan Xaramillo's second wife, Beatriz de Andrade, who was, it seemed, related to Doña Margarita de Peralta. Xaramillo had been dead more than twenty years by the time of this investigation in 1570, but Doña Beatriz had been very young when she married him, so she was probably in her fifties when she swore her statement to the Inquisition. In it she made mention of Malinche as Xaramillo's 'first and legitimate wife', but otherwise there was nothing of any use to me, no dates, no reference to the cause of her death.

In the second volume I found a parchment dated 1609 relating to Fernando Cortés. 'Fernando Cortés' it was headed, *'casado dos veces'*, 'married twice'. So it was an accusation of bigamy. The words were written in a slender hand across the top right-hand corner, and *'casado'* was spelled *'cafado'* with that familiar transposition of 'f' for 's' common in English documents of this period too.

Captain Justino Sanchez de Sosa accused Fernando Cortés of marrying first one woman in Seville and then, while she was still alive, a second woman in Lima, who was now living with him in Mexico City. There was no reference to his ancestry, but the details of this life were familiar to me. There had been a sojourn in Lima, a subsequent residence in Mexico City. I was certain this man was Malinche's grandson, the son of her child, Martin Cortés.

There was nothing to indicate the outcome of the denunciation, nor Fernando Cortés's eventual fate. Sanchez de Sosa declared in self-righteous fashion that he was bringing this information to the Inquisition's notice 'as an obedient son of the Church', and it was poignant to see Malinche's grandson treading on such dangerous ground. However there was nothing more to assist me in my search for her.

I knew the connection had been fragile. I had not really expected to find the answers I wanted in these old Inquisition testimonies. It is just that when searching for a woman like Malinche, you become accustomed to leaving no stone unturned.

aftermath

· · ·

Later that week, in my room at the pension, I began work on the papers from Seville which Filomena Alvarado had kept for me while I was travelling on the Isthmus. They were photocopies of documents recording a twenty-year legal battle in the Xaramillo family.

In 1542 Malinche's daughter Maria Xaramillo was sixteen and newly married to the viceroy's nephew, Luis de Quesada. In terms of rank it should have been a brilliant marriage for a young *mestiza* like her, and yet there is evidence to suggest that she married Quesada against her will. The evidence comes from an interesting quarter: from Hernan Cortés himself. In an interrogatory he swore soon after Maria Xaramillo's marriage Cortés claimed that the viceroy, Don Antonio Mendoza, had forced Maria into marriage with his nephew against her will and that of her father. Cortés stated that Quesada, with the help of the viceroy's servants, had climbed the walls of Xaramillo's house and abducted Maria. Quesada, according to Cortés, had then claimed publicly that they were married and caused Maria Xaramillo so many problems, *le hizo tantas molestias*, that she was obliged to marry him.

This extraordinary story of the abduction of Malinche's daughter by the viceroy's nephew is limited to one small paragraph in a long set of interrogatories. What are we to make of it? Was Luis de Quesada driven by a violent obsession with Maria Xaramillo? Or, given that her father was by now one of the richest men in the colony, was it the thought of her potential inheritance that drove him to kidnap her? Or did Cortés invent the entire story to discredit the family of his bitter enemy, the viceroy?

Whatever the truth of the matter, whatever Maria Xaramillo's attitude to her aristocratic husband, in 1542 the two of them commenced legal proceedings against her father, Juan Xaramillo. They had learned that he intended to leave Maria only one third of his estate and the rest to his second wife Beatriz de Andrade.

Maria Xaramillo began her evidence to the Royal Audiencia with a long, formal letter, followed by a series of sworn testimonies of former conquistadors who claimed that they had known Maria's mother, 'the famous indian, doña Marina'.

Maria's legitimacy was essential to her claim on her father's property, so the witnesses began by swearing that her parents had been married according to the rites of the Holy Church. Next they attested to Malinche's 'good service and fidelity' during the wars of conquest. They praised her intelligence, her sagacity, her courage, and the high esteem with which she was held by the 'indians'.

Many of the witnesses were familiar to me, such as Juan de Orteguilla, who as a pageboy had learned Nahuatl at Malinche's side and served Moctezuma in his imprisonment. But two important names were missing from these testimonies. Bernal Diaz was resident far away in Guatemala, and Geronimo de Aguilar had been dead for several years.

The witnesses commended Malinche's linguistic skills and the intelligence role she played, and several of them referred specifically to her death. 'After the death of doña Marina,' they said, 'Maria had been raised in Xaramillo's house.' Or 'the said doña Marina died' and Maria grew up in Xaramillo's house.

Is there something odd about these statements? Where else would we expect Maria to have been raised? Do the words of these witnesses suggest that before her mother's death the child had not been living with her father?

Among the Xaramillo–Quesada papers was a statement sworn by Maria Xaramillo herself. After her mother's death, she said, her father, 'the said Juan Xaramillo', married a second time, to Doña Beatriz de Andrade 'by whom he has had no other son or daughter even though they have been married twenty years'.

I returned to the first paragraph of Maria Xaramillo's statement and saw that it was dated 29 March 1547. So if Juan Xaramillo and Beatriz de Andrade had been married twenty years when Maria swore this document, Malinche must have been dead by 1527. She would have been around twenty-seven years old, and Maria herself would barely have been two. She would scarcely have known her mother.

❦

The Archivo Historico of Mexico City is housed in a beautiful eighteenth-century mansion on Calle Republica de Chile. 'Here the memory of the City of Mexico is guarded,' I read on the plaque at the entrance as I passed through the massive doors into a shaded cloister, as elegant and tranquil as the interior of a monastery.

The librarian asked if I would prefer to read from the printed editions or from the originals on microfilm. I chose the unexpected luxury of the printed texts and waited while he disappeared among the shelves to find them. Then I carried the heavy, bound volumes for the years 1521–29 and 1530–39 to a table by the window where the light was good.

Outside the cars and buses roared along the street while I sat there reading the earliest minutes, the *Actas*, of the fledgling town council of Mexico City, when it was still called Temystitan-Mexico, in a mangled echo of its former name. It was strange to come across familiar characters and know they had survived. I felt that I had followed them from one end of a long tunnel to the other.

There was Isabel Rodriguez, one of the women who had come with Cortés's fleet and was renowned for her skills as a healer: 'the famous woman who cured wounds during the wars of Conquest', the records called her. According to the entry for 17 November 1525, Isabel Rodriguez was granted a plot of land for a garden behind her house. The following day Geronimo de Aguilar, married by now to an Amerindian woman from Topoyanco called Elvira Toznenitzin, was also granted land for a garden.

Juan Xaramillo appeared frequently in the records, for he was already a wealthy and prominent citizen of Temystitan-Mexico, and on February 1528 he was made lieutenant of the city. A few weeks later, on Saturday 14 March, there was, at last, a brief reference to Malinche. 'To Juan Xaramillo,' the notation read, 'and to his wife doña Marina', a grant of land in the woodland beside the wall of Chapultepec, where they could run sheep.

So the council believed Malinche was alive in March 1528. There was a discrepancy here, for in 1547 Maria Xaramillo believed that her father had been remarried for twenty years. But the discrepancy was slight and not unreasonable if Maria was so very young when her mother died.

By noon the reading room was full of students from the university. They had their own concerns, researching other moments in their city's life. I asked the librarian if I could now see the microfilm of the original document.

On the screen before me I stared at the spindly letters which had been scratched so meticulously onto the parchment all those centuries ago. There was something compelling about the original handwriting, even if only on microfilm. *Juan Xaramillo e a doña Marina su mujer . . . un sytio . . . en la arboleda . . . a la pared de Chapultepec.* It occurred to me that this was the only time I had ever seen Malinche referred to as a living person, and not just a memory.

I spent the rest of that afternoon going carefully through the records for the next twenty years. There are references to Juan Xaramillo throughout that year, on 4 April, 22 June, 14 August. But after 14 March 1528 there is not another word about Malinche.

Sixteenth-century Mexico was a society without divorce, where bigamy was dangerous. There was always some enemy or rival willing to denounce you to the Church authorities, as Malinche's grandson, Fernando Cortés, had discovered in 1609. Xaramillo's marriage to Malinche, whatever its hidden flaws, had been conducted by a distinguished priest in front of witnesses, and was considered by the society in which they lived to have been a formal union.

It is most unlikely that Xaramillo could have remarried while

Malinche was alive. So if Maria Xaramillo believed that by 1547 her father and his second wife had been married for twenty years, Malinche must have died soon after that final entry in March 1528.

In Mexico City, between 1527 and 1532, there were many ways to die. If you were a Spaniard you might be denounced as a Jew by some enemy you had made on your way to prosperity, as was the former conquistador Hernando Alonso. This unfortunate man was burned at the stake in 1528.

There were mysterious stomach complaints that claimed many lives among the Spanish community at this time. There were also a number of notable deaths that provoked whisperings about poison or foul play: Cortés's first wife, for example, who perished in his house in Coyoacan, and later two representatives of the Spanish Crown who dined with him and died soon after. As for women residents, whatever their race they faced the usual hazards of pregnancy and childbirth. But for Amerindian residents of the city a sudden and hideous death was a thousand times more likely than for Spaniards. After the Conquest wave after lethal wave of smallpox, chickenpox, mumps and measles, engulfed the Culua-Mexica survivors, killing them in their tens of thousands.

It is hardly surprising therefore that the many witnesses who testified that Malinche was dead did not bother to mention how she died. In the context of all this horror, what was one more death? The remarkable thing about Malinche is that she survived as long as she did.

In 1528, shortly after the town council made that final grant of land to Malinche and Juan Xaramillo, Hernan Cortés departed for Spain. He took with him a large entourage of Culua-Mexica and Tlaxcalan nobles to present at the royal court, and he also took Malinche's child, Martin, who was then about six years old.

There is no evidence that Malinche went with Cortés on this well-documented journey, and if she had accompanied him her presence would surely have been noted. However, the departure of her small son and her erstwhile protector coincides very closely with her disappearance from the council records. So did the loss of her child crush her spirit and hasten her end in that disease-stricken city?

Since the day she was taken from Jaltipan, Malinche had stood alone outside society, belonging nowhere, living on her wits, relying on the personal courage which so astonished Bernal Diaz. For a few short years from 1519 to 1526 she had played a role crucial enough to safeguard her survival, but all that was finished now. She had no formal power base. She was not the daughter of an honoured family as was Isabel de Moctezuma. Apart from that small allotment beside the wall in the woodland of Chapultepec, she had no property that we know of. All she had left, if she had them at all, were her infant daughter Maria and her husband Juan Xaramillo, on whose goodwill she was now entirely dependent.

The nature of Malinche's relationship with this man remains concealed from us, but the stories of his drunkenness at Orizaba are not encouraging, in spite of Bernal Diaz's denials. Nor is

Xaramillo's perplexing attempt to disinherit Maria Xaramillo. Maria was his only child, yet he seems to have felt little filial tenderness for her.

Does the interest that Hernan Cortés showed in Maria Xaramillo's marriage suggest that she was really his daughter? Perhaps Xaramillo suspected this, which is why he behaved the way he did toward Maria? Yet Cortés, as far as we can tell, usually acknowledged his illegitimate children and made provision for them in his will, even when their mothers were the wives of other men. So if Maria Xaramillo were his daughter, why would he not have acknowledged her too?

Whatever the truth, the shadow of a loveless, bitter marriage lingers over Malinche's final years. In such a city, ridden with disease and suffering, it must have been easy for someone, even someone as notable as she was, simply to disappear.

There are stories, inevitable stories, that after Cortés left for Spain Xaramillo abandoned Malinche. Or that he had her murdered and her body disposed of in one of the city's canals. Or that she made her way back to Jaltipan to die. But no conclusive evidence has come to light to confirm these speculations. All we can say is that Malinche died sometime after March 1528, probably in one of the great and horrifying plagues that were sweeping Mexico at that time. And that like the hundreds of thousands of other Amerindian men and women who perished during those terrible years following the Conquest, she was buried in an unmarked grave.

aftermath

. . .

ry corner in the old quarter of Mexico City there
and ancient church. Their walls are rent with
ed cracks and many may not survive another great
ome will eventually be closed to ensure public
safety, like the old Basilica of Guadalupe, which has now been
replaced by a large modern chapel.

On the corner of Pino Suarez I found the Iglesia de Jesus
Nazarene. It is one of the earliest Spanish churches in Mexico
City. I stepped into the dark interior. It was very bare, very
simple, and I loved its quiet austerity: stone floor, plain stone
walls, no elaborate carvings, nothing but the glow of candles on
the altar. I sat in the back pew as people came and went, making
their silent devotions, kneeling, praying, genuflecting, crossing
themselves with great solemnity.

Halfway up the side aisle, sitting in a little booth with his
hands folded sedately on the bench in front of him, was an altar
boy. I went over and, whispering, I asked him if this was the
place where Hernan Cortés's remains were buried. He looked up
at me with dark and serious eyes. He was very young, probably
no more than seven or eight. 'Yes, señora,' he said, and he
pointed toward the altar. 'His vault is up there, on the left-hand
side, in the wall.'

I walked along the narrow aisle toward the front of the church
and saw the vault set high in the wall. It was covered by a modest
plaque inscribed with just a name and set of dates: 'Hernan
Cortés 1485–1547.'

Cortés returned to Spain in 1528 a wealthy man. He married

an aristocratic wife, took her back to Mexico and had several children by her, including the second Martin Cortés, his heir. In his lifetime Cortés achieved everything except the very thing he most desired: to become the governor or viceroy of the lands he had conquered. He was far too much of an adventurer for the Crown to entrust him with such a role.

In 1540 he returned to Spain where he died seven years later. His body was initially buried near Seville, but in 1566 it was exhumed and taken to Mexico by his son, the legitimate Martin Cortés. After their arrival in Mexico his remains were exhumed and reinterred on at least seven more occasions.

During the independence wars against Spain in the nineteenth century, threats were made to drag Cortés's bones through the streets and burn them on a ceremonial pyre. They were once more exhumed and this time they went missing for an entire century. When they were rediscovered in 1946, plans were made for their formal reinterrment the following year in the Iglesia de Jesus Nazarene.

So after four centuries of wandering from crypt to crypt, Cortés's bones were finally laid to rest in this small, simple church constructed on the very same part of the old causeway where Moctezuma had greeted him in 1519. Among those present at the little ceremony on 9 July 1947 was the scholar Federico Gomez de Orozco. As a direct descendant of Cortés and Malinche, he had come to witness his ancestor's burial.

Cortés is still despised in Mexico. But his remains have rested quietly in this church for more than fifty years now, which for Cortés is a long time. It is many years since anyone has threatened to drag them from their vault and desecrate them. Since independence from Spain was achieved they have lost their symbolic value and no one much cares about them anymore.

Bernal Diaz del Castillo was only twenty-five years old in 1521 when Tenochtitlan finally fell. After that he settled for a while in the Coatzocoalcos district, where Malinche had been born, but eventually he moved south to the beautiful city of Antigua in Guatemala. He married a Spanish wife and kept a Mayan mistress as well, by whom he had several children.

He was seventy-two years old when he completed the first draft of his memoirs, which he pointedly called, 'The True History of the Conquest of New Spain', to differentiate it from the academic histories, which to his disgust were attracting such popularity in Spain. Only he had been there, only he had seen it all with his own eyes. This was the story he wanted to tell. He sent his manuscript to Spain in 1575, but he never saw it published: that did not occur until almost halfway through the next century.

The little house in Antigua in which Bernal Diaz lived and wrote his memoirs is still there. It is a school these days, or it was the last time I saw it, early in 1974. Diaz was always a more modest man than his commander. He lived the rest of his life in Guatemala with his family around him, and died at the extraordinary age for that time of eighty-eight. As far as I know his bones still rest undisturbed in Antigua, beneath the shadow of its three volcanoes.

Until her own death in the late 1560s, Malinche's daughter, Maria Xaramillo, is believed to have spent many hours of every day praying in the Holy Trinity Church, La Santisima Trinidad, in Mexico City. La Santisima, as it is always affectionately known, stands four blocks west of Mexico City's central plaza, in the small street that bears its name, la Calle de la Santisima. I asked Filomena if she would come with me to see it.

'This is what we call the *churriguera* style, or Mexican baroque,' Filomena said proudly as she showed me the elaborate carving of its wooden doors with their intricate swirls and spirals. 'La Santisima is one of the most beautiful examples of *churriguera* in all of Mexico City.'

Earlier that day, in the Archivo Historico, I had copied out some notes on the history of La Santisima. According to the council records it had been established in 1526 as a hermitage with a hospice attached. It was a place where the poor and needy, *los pobres e miserables*, could be cared for.

'The church was still a hospice in the days when Maria Xaramillo came here to pray,' I whispered to Filomena. 'Do you suppose she believed that her mother had died here? Is that what inspired Maria's devotion to this church?'

'It is possible,' Filomena replied. 'If Malinche were dying from smallpox, if Xaramillo had cast her out onto the streets, perhaps she could have made her way here. Where else could she have gone?'

At the altar two young boys moved about in silence, lighting long, tapering candles. 'It says here,' Filomena was reading quietly from my notes, 'that during the seventeenth century the original Santisima was used as a home for demented priests. But that eventually it became too dangerous and had to be demolished.'

'Does nothing remain of the original church?' I asked her.

'No, apparently nothing.'

We stood there in silence as worshippers came and went with heads bowed, crossing themselves, touching their crucifixes to their lips.

'Nothing is left,' Filomena said quietly. 'So if Malinche died here, if her bones were laid to rest within these walls . . .' I looked around at the flowers, the glowing candles, 'they would have been pounded into dust centuries ago, beneath these great stone foundations.'

IV

mythologies

From legends men draw ideas
necessary for their existence.

ANATOLE FRANCE

Avatar

Malinche died but she was never truly laid to rest. She became a silent river into which the memories of the great pre-Hispanic female divinities began to trickle, intermingling slowly, gathering momentum as they went.

The Tlaxcalans gave her name to the volcano they had formerly associated with the jade-skirted goddess Matlecueye. On the gulf coast, close to where Malinche spent her years in slavery, the Maya named the stream running into the sea in her honour. On the Isthmus of Tehuantepec the story that she had made her solitary way back there to die, that she was entombed beneath that burial mound in Jaltipan gained currency.

Slowly the Malinche dances with all their intricate variations began to evolve. In some villages the Malinche character would be played by either a young girl or a young boy. In others the Malinche was a man in woman's costume, a curious transvestite figure complete with male–female mask: a living emblem of human fertility. Sometimes the Malinche figure exhibited sorrow for her part in the Conquest. In other variations she was the harbinger, rather than the agent, of catastrophe.

In the Malinche dance around Jaltipan she was represented by two little girls, one called Marina, the other La Moctezuma. 'Awake, King, from your heavy dream,' the small Malinches warn their husband, the Emperor. 'See that they will capture you while you are sleeping.' But Moctezuma takes no notice and the dance ends with his death and the crowning of a new king who will play his role the following year. In Jaltipan the Malinche dance has become a ritual of death and resurrection.

After her death Malinche lived on among the indigenous communities of New Spain in a multitude of such acts of remembrance. Even while she was still alive she joined the world of ghosts for one ephemeral moment. It happened late in 1525 while she was far away on the journey to Honduras. A Spaniard passing a square in Tenochtitlan claimed to see her spirit burning there, beside that of Cortés. The man told everyone it meant they had died in Honduras, but he was wrong. To his great embarrassment they returned early the following year.

But that fleeting episode belongs to the Spanish branch of Malinche's story. The Amerindian side of her mythology, its origins, its strange coalescence with older beliefs, is a more complex journey through ambiguity and duplication, through endlessly reflecting mirrors.

⚜

I started going to the Museo Nacional de Antropologia in the Bosque de Chapultepec every morning. I would take the bus from the statue of tragic Cuauhtemoc, or sometimes I would walk, making my way through the silent crowds of Mayans from Chiapas protesting beside the statue of the Angel of Independence. The traffic along the Avenida de la Reforma was deafening, and I was always glad to slip through the iron gates of the park into the quiet of its gardens.

The parcel of land the early town council had granted to Malinche and Xaramillo in 1528 'beside the wall of Chapultepec' had been somewhere within these woodlands. Long after her death, even as late as the nineteenth century, people still claimed to have glimpsed her walking silently among the trees.

Chapultepec is no longer the luxuriant forest it once was, but it endures somehow in the brown and stifling atmosphere, where the only rain that falls is acid rain. And every Sunday families still come in their thousands to picnic on the dry grass beneath its ancient trees.

Upstairs, on the first floor of the Museo, I would spend the day reading, looking out across the parkland from time to time, trying to find my way through the labyrinth that is pre-Conquest mythology. I knew the references to Malinche's spirit walking and weeping in the night had a pre-Hispanic connection, and I was curious to see if I could trace its derivation. It wasn't easy. There is nothing simple about the Culua-Mexica pantheon, no crisply defined gods and goddesses assigned exclusively to this or that role. But of all the female divinities it is Cihuacoatl, 'Woman Serpent', who is the most complex and polymorphic.

She did not originate with the Culua-Mexica. That is to say, her myth had not come with them on their long migratory journey south from Aztlan, the place of the white-feathered heron. Cihuacoatl belonged to the older civilisations of the Valley of Mexico; she had been their patron for centuries. But around 1430, as the Culua-Mexica laid waste the last of those ancient cities, they appropriated the cult of Cihuacoatl. From that day on they claimed her as their own.

I found a thought-provoking essay by an art historian called Cecilia Klein. In 'Rethinking Cihuacoatl' Klein described the numerous stone images of Cihuacoatl and her many avatars. The placement of the goddess at the base of those intricate carvings, her nakedness, her decapitation, suggested to Klein that in the early years of her appropriation, Cihuacoatl's image as a captive woman was crucial to the Culua-Mexica. Her violation, her desecration, became the ultimate symbol of their ascendancy over the older cities they had conquered.

The rape of women in war has been so rarely acknowledged and so rarely documented that the Culua-Mexica's explicit use of such a symbol is shocking to our twentieth-century sensibilities. But Cihuacoatl later acquired other attributes and other manifestations in the hearts and minds of the Culua-Mexica.

She could be terrifying in her guise as Coatlicue, 'Serpent Skirt', courageous as Yoacihuatl, 'Warrior Woman', benevolent as Quilatzli, the patron of midwives. Eventually the Culua-Mexica gave her name to their second highest political position, so that from the middle of the fifteenth century onward, the man who advised the *Tlatoani*, the Speaker, became known as the *Cihuacoatl*.

Cihuacoatl, the divinity, was known for one particularly

terrifying activity however. At night she went walking. She would weep and wail and cry aloud for her children, striking terror into the hearts of all who heard her. Her chilling lament was interpreted, always, as a sign of impending disaster.

Some ideas can never be eradicated, no matter how many edicts and injunctions are imposed by Church or State. Instead they alter their shape through the ages, subtly, almost imperceptibly, the way a bird or animal evolves and mutates over time in order to survive. We call it folk memory, race memory, cultural memory. Whatever name we choose to give it, we should know by now that it is indestructible.

After the Conquest the indigenous residents of what was now New Spain still heard a woman weeping in the night, crying out for her children; but they no longer said it was Cihuacoatl, probably because the Christian friars had forbidden the use of the goddess's name. Instead they chose another name for their ancient phantom, a safer, more anonymous title: *La Llorona*, the 'Weeping Woman'.

Indigenous and *mestizo* Mexicans have never ceased to hear her. Sometimes, as I knew from my conversations with the iguana seller in Jaltipan and the children in Malinche's house, they associate her with Malinche. As if somewhere, at some unrecorded moment, when Malinche had been dead for who knows how long, she slipped like a sorrowful avatar into Cihuacoatl's place in popular memory. She inherited the goddess's pain, the inconsolable and universal grief of a woman who has lost her children.

If you walk from the metropolitan cathedral in Mexico City to the Plaza de Santo Domingo just a few blocks away, you will pass the former site of Cihuacoatl's temple. It once stood somewhere near the corner of Calle República de Brasil and Calle Justo Sierra, among the cafes and bakeries where the shopkeepers sweep their pavements so industriously each morning.

Soon after the Conquest a small boy called Diego Duran arrived in Tenochtitlan from Spain with his parents. Like many of his peers he grew up speaking both Spanish and Nahuatl. He later recalled that in those early years after the fall of Tenochtitlan, the ruins of Cihuacoatl's temple remained untouched, a desolate reminder of the final siege. He said that he and the other Spanish boys used to peer into its shadowy interior and dare each other to enter this place they called the 'Devil's House' with its terrifying stone idols still buried in the debris.

Diego Duran eventually became a Dominican priest, and one of the fathers of modern ethnology. He devoted his life to recording the myths and legends of the Culua-Mexica whom he considered to be his spiritual flock. In the library of the Museo Nacional de Antropologia I found his famous *Book of the Gods and Rites of the Ancient Calendar* with its scholarly descriptions of the numerous pre-Conquest deities. All the great divinities were represented, the mythology of each one laid out in neat, biographical style, like a pagan *Lives of Saints*.

I came to his account of Malinalxochitl, 'Wild Grass Flower'. I saw the elegant letters spread out across the page to form that beautiful, extravagant name, and I noted its similarity to Malinche's. According to Duran, Malinalxochitl's legend dated from the years when the people who became the Culua-Mexica were still barbarians wandering in the wilderness, before they descended into the Valley of Mexico and established their great city, Tenochtitlan.

Malinalxochitl was one of the tribe's leaders as they began their long migratory journey south. But at some point along the way conflict and discord erupted among them, and they split into two camps. One half of the tribe departed with Malinalxochitl, the other remained with her brother Huitzilopochtli, who would later become the supreme deity of the Culua-Mexica.

After this schism Malinalxochitl and her followers became the first of their people to found a city. They called it Malinalco in her honour, and it still stands 25 kilometres south-west of Mexico City. But the split did not heal relations between sister and brother and their respective followers. Hostilities intensified until eventually Malinalxochitl's son, Copil, led a great war against his uncle. It was fought out in a series of savage battles along the shores of the lake in the Valley of Mexico. Copil was defeated and, as he lay dying his uncle Huitzilopochtli tore out his beating heart, held it on high for all to see, then flung it far out into the marshes of the lake.

Huitzilopochtli and his followers watched as it descended into the water. As it did a cactus sprang up on which a mighty eagle landed, clasping a serpent in its beak. The bird moved its head up and down slowly and called to them: 'O Mexica it shall be here.' That was when they knew their wanderings had finally ended. On this island in the lake they would build a great city of their own and call it Tenochtitlan, 'Cactus Rock'.

The lights had been turned on inside the library. It was not yet evening but the rain clouds gathering over the city had darkened the sky. Students and scholars moved around quietly, collecting books, making notes, engaged in whispered conversations, while I sat there contemplating the legend of Malinalxochitl.

Like Malinche she had been an agent of destruction. Like Malinche she had been instrumental in the founding of a new city. Malinalxochitl's name was derived from the glyph for wild grass, as was Malinche's purported Amerindian name: Malinalli. This glyph, as delicate as a butterfly, reveals a curious ambiguity on close inspection. It was intended to represent grass waving in the wind, and yet, to the twentieth-century eye it can also look like an elegant feathered headdress. At certain angles it resembles the lower jaw of a skull — a frequent symbol for Cihuacoatl, Woman Serpent.

Similar threads of exile, of dissent and disinheritance in Malinalxochitl's legend were present in Malinche's story. How many of these parallels were coincidence? How many were intentionally constructed or unconsciously reinforced by Culua-Mexica survivors, as a way of making sense of Malinche and the part she had played in the calamity she had suffered?

I thought about Malinalxochitl frequently after that. It occurred to me that if Moctezuma had truly been inclined to mistake one of the conquistadors for a returning god, it should logically have been Malinche, not Cortés, who caused him such supposed terror and despair. With her powerful resemblance in name and deed to his ancestor-goddess Malinalxochitl, Malinche would have made a perfect candidate.

But what we call history can be a capricious and highly selective affair. The early Franciscan evangelists, to whom we are indebted for the enduring story of the returning god Quetzalcoatl and his association with Cortés, seem to have taken little notice of the myth of Malinalxochitl. Like all Meso American goddesses she was far removed from the sanitised virgins of Christian theology, and it is difficult to see what use the Franciscans could have had for such a complex female figure in their teachings. It is possible, however, that if they had devoted serious thought to her legend, our popular understanding of the Conquest of Mexico might have evolved quite differently.

Through the library windows I watched people running through the pouring rain toward the buses and taxis waiting along the avenue outside. It was too wet to leave, so I went downstairs to the Mexica Room of the Museo. I stood before the colossal basalt statue of one of Cihuacoatl's avatars, Coatlicue, 'Serpent Skirt'. She loomed above me, terrifying in her necklace of severed human hands and hearts, her skirt of writhing snakes.

Her statue was discovered late in the eighteenth century by workmen doing drainage repairs in the central plaza of Mexico City. She was excavated and dragged to the university, examined by a panel of learned men, measured, sketched, documented and swiftly reburied in secret. The city fathers feared the sight of her might rekindle the flames of the old religion in the hearts of their indigenous subjects.

Thirteen years later when the great German archaeologist Alexander von Humboldt visited Mexico City, he arranged for Coatlicue to be exhumed. As soon as he had examined her, however, the authorities buried her once more. But times change. Now Coatlicue dominates the Mexica Room with her terrible beauty. She is cherished as an object of sculptural grandeur by all those who come to see her, and as a symbol of the glorious Amerindian past.

When Ignacio Bernal was director of the Museo Nacional de Antropologia at Chapultepec, he remarked that in Mexico even archaeological artefacts are subject to the dictates of changing fashion. Coatlicue, with her burials and exhumations, is a perfect example of what he meant.

So what happened to Malinche's image in the nineteenth century at the hands of Mexico's small but powerful white elite was probably inevitable. She was a woman whose name everybody knew, but about whom almost nothing was known. That is why it must have been easy, when the time was right, to cut the cloth and reconfigure her to fit a new and less forgiving mythology.

Traitor

For as long as I can remember I have known that one man's renegade is another's hero. When I was growing up in the 1960s, Mohammed Ali was vilified as a traitor in the United States because he refused to fight what he saw as a white man's war in Vietnam. In Australia during the First World War, Irish immigrants like my grandfather who refused to fight for their old enemy, Britain, suffered similar abuse. In the closing months of 1998 Chileans who supported Augusto Pinochet's extradition from England to Spain on charges of torture and murder were denounced as traitors to their country. Examples of the innate subjectivity of treachery are never difficult to find.

I no longer recall at what point I began to question the validity of Malinche's image as a traitor. But I know my scepticism grew as I made my way through the documents, the painted books, the linguistic maps, as I listened to stories and legends, as I journeyed through Mexico that summer, crossing and recrossing the old political and cultural boundaries that had once divided this ancient land.

If there was a moment of revelation it occurred when I realised that in the indigenous histories prepared in the aftermath of the Conquest, Malinche is never referred to as a traitor, not even in the Florentine Codex with its Culua-Mexica perspective. Malinche was an enemy, along with the Spaniards, the Tlaxcalans, the Huejotzingans. But the word 'traitor' suggests a different kind of enemy, an enemy within, and there was no evidence in Culua-Mexica writings that they ever considered her in such a light.

There was a long and curious gap between Malinche's death and her demonisation as Mexico's national villain. That process did not begin until three hundred years after her death, and when it did it coincided with the rise of Mexican nationalism in the early years of the nineteenth century. I should have guessed it would be like that. It is usually in the throes of nationalist fervour that societies seek to construct and reconstruct their heroes and villains. But Malinche's fall from grace is a strange and paradoxical story because the voices that rose to denounce her for her supposed treachery in siding with the Spaniards during the Conquest were not the voices of indigenous or *mestizo* Mexicans. The denunciations came from European voices; from the numerically small but influential white elite of pure Spanish ancestry that had dominated political and economic life in the colony since the Conquest: the *criollos*.

It is difficult to say who among this privileged sector of Mexican society was the first to remember Malinche, for the *criollos* had previously shown little interest in this long-dead

Amerindian woman. They did not hear her weeping in the night. They did not take part in the Malinche dances. They had probably never heard of Malinalxochitl. The *criollos* yearned, understandably, to be free of Spanish rule, but they had remained entirely Spanish in their cultural orientation.

Their attitude to Malinche is exemplified in a speech made by one of Mexico's most eloquent nationalists at a ceremony to commemorate his country's declaration of independence from Spain in 1821. 'It is one of the mysteries of fate,' he declared, 'that all nations owe their fall and ignominy to a woman.'

He could have invoked the names of Eve, of Helen of Troy, even of Malinalxochitl if he preferred a Mexican example. But the distinguished guests who listened to him speak that day knew he had a particular woman in his sights. It was Malinche of course. She was a Mexican Eve, he told them. She had caused her people to be driven from the Garden of Eden.

The speaker's name was Ignacio Ramirez. He was a man of Spanish ancestry, yet as his speech proceeded he lamented the conquest of Tenochtitlan as if the people of that doomed city had been his own forebears. Why did he do this? Because he was indulging in a little ancestor borrowing. As politicians do, he was reconfiguring history to suit his own ideological purposes.

It was important to Mexican nationalists as they broke from the Spanish Crown, to seek legitimacy through another kind of ancient lineage. They turned to the Mexican past for that essential link. But the past they embraced had been cleansed of all its pre-Conquest complexity, and was inhabited by only one people: the Culua-Mexica of Tenochtitlan. If the Independence leaders understood the kaleidoscope of indigenous cultures that had characterised pre-Hispanic Mexico, and continued to do so even in the nineteenth century, they did not acknowledge them. The truth would have ruined the fashionable symmetry of the nationalist argument: that the vast and newly declared Republic of Mexico was a restoration of the Culua-Mexica empire.

This then was how Malinche's reinvention as a traitor came about — through this sad distortion of the Mexican past. She had been an enemy of the Culua-Mexica. It followed therefore that she was also an enemy of the new nation of Mexico. But Ignacio Ramirez's speech makes it clear that Malinche's malevolent image was fashioned by more atavistic forces than mere politics or patriotism. It depended also on an ancient and familiar belief in the general perfidy of women. That, presumably, is why the notion of Malinche's treachery was so easily assimilated into the hearts and minds of Mexican nationalists. As Ramirez said, all nations owed their fall to a woman, and everybody knew this. Malinche was a traitor to her country in a way the warriors of Tlaxcala could never be, simply because she was a woman.

In a bookstore on Avenida Madero I asked the sales manager if he had any works on his shelves about Malinche.

'Malinche?' he pursed his lips and regarded me with disapproval. 'I don't believe so.'

But there was one slender volume. Its cover caught my eye, with its beautiful sepia reproduction of a plate from the *Lienzo de Tlaxcala*, a scene in which Malinche accepts gifts of woven blankets from a group of young Tlaxcalan women.

The book was entitled *La Malinche in Mexican Literature* by Sandra Messinger Cypess, and it had found its way onto the shelves in spite of the manager's disdain. Its presence was miraculous, but its price was high and I agonised over it for some time, because my money was running short by now. In the end I purchased it and took it back to my room at the pension to read. I turned to the chapter dealing with the nationalist era, a chapter Cypess had adroitly titled 'Eve and the Serpent'.

The novels and plays she described had beautiful evocative names such as *The Martyrs of Anahuac* and *Xicontencatl*. A hatred of all things Spanish was fundamental to their plots, as we would expect given the time when they were written, and they were peopled by real historic figures: Cortés, Cuauhtemoc, Juan Xaramillo, and most importantly, Malinche.

There is a rule of thumb in art and literature. If you wish to subvert a man's reputation you deform him physically. You cripple him and endow him with a hunchback, as Shakespeare did with Richard III, or paint him syphillitic with an imbecile's drool, as Diego Rivera did with Hernan Cortés in several of his murals. If you wish to attack a woman, you do so through her sexuality. It was in the literature of the nationalist era, therefore, that a new dimension of sexual depravity was added to the legend of 'Malinche's political treachery'.

Her lascivious nature was sometimes emphasised in those curious nineteenth-century morality tales by the interpolation into the plot of a fictional Amerindian noblewoman. This paragon of virtue would reject Cortés's advances, while the insatiable Malinche went about her vile business, attempting to seduce a mind-numbing procession of real and fictitious men: Cortés, Puertocarrero, Diego de Ordaz, even Cuauhtemoc.

There is not the slightest evidence to support those fantasies about Malinche's promiscuity. Not the smallest scrap of gossip from Bernal Diaz, who was an ardent gossip. Not one word from the many witnesses who testified about Cortés's sexual habits during the *Residencia,* nor from those who gave evidence about Malinche in Maria Xaramillo's law suit. Not even from those who came forward on behalf of Maria's stepmother, witnesses who had good reason to slander Malinche's name. Yet the notion of Malinche's sexual deviance that emerged from the pages of those imaginative nineteenth-century works has become integral to the legend of her treachery. It has permeated well beyond the realm of nineteenth-century Mexican literature.

When English author Gary Jennings wrote his best-selling novel *Aztec* in the early 1980s, he gave his hero, Mixtli, several unpleasant sexual encounters with Malinche. When she first attempts to seduce him she is still little more than a child. The noble Mixtli is horrified by her lewdness and resists her with manly virtue. 'I have known other females like you,' he tells her, 'venal and deceitful and perfidious.'

Jennings follows the traditional pattern of providing us with a virtuous female with whom we may compare the depraved Malinche. In this case it is Mixtli's daughter, and to add to the piquancy of the comparison she too is called Malinalli. But she dies tragically young, and in his sorrow her grieving father, Mixtli, warns the evil Malinalli [Malinche] that she will make the name she shares with his dead child 'vile and filthy and contemptible and all people will spit when they speak it'.

The last time Mixtli sees Malinche her hair is dyed red, 'like that of the whores of Santiago de Cuba'. She has become what he predicted at that first meeting: 'a red-haired slut who has sold more than just her own body to the invader'.

What would the real Malinche make of all this? The Maya gave her to Cortés for the purposes of concubinage, and she would have known what was expected of her. She had no reason to resist her fate, and no chance on earth of preventing it. If she had realised in her brief and precarious lifetime that she would one day be condemned for her intimacy with this man she would probably have been perplexed and bewildered. Or perhaps she might have laughed. In the context of her predicament, it would have made no sense to her at all.

Anyone who crosses from the United States to Mexico recognises immediately that some curious racial experiment unfamiliar in the British colonial experience has occurred in this older Iberian empire. In Spanish it is called '*mestizaje*', in English 'miscegenation'. In Mexico *mestizaje* is an everyday word because it describes the majority of Mexican people. In English the term 'miscegenation' is rarely called for.

In Mexico you see the visual manifestation of *mestizaje* in the gracefully oblique cast of Mexican eyes, in the hawk-like curve of the nose, in the traditional Spanish names attached to 'indian' countenances. And if you listen carefully you can hear the linguistic result of *mestizaje* in Mexican Spanish, with its vast lexical borrowings from Nahuatl.

When cultures meet for the first time the most immediate and urgent linguistic borrowing occurs in the obvious realm of previously unknown things: fruits and plants, birds and animals, indigenous weaponry and artefacts. Words such as *boomerang* and *woomera* are typical English borrowings from indigenous Australian languages. These borrowings occurred because English had no immediately appropriate words for the objects in question.

As we would expect, Mexican Spanish exhibits this typical category of Nahuatl loan-words for new and unfamiliar things, especially for the extraordinary plants and foods of the New World. Many of these loan-words even passed through Spanish into English in the years following the Conquest. Words like chocolate from *chocolatl*, tomato from *tomatl*, avocado from *awuacatl*, and countless others.

But Mexican Spanish also embraced thousands of Nahuatl words for objects that were already familiar to the Spanish conquerors. It is not just the remarkable quantity of such loan-words, but their broad and far-reaching nature, which is striking. Words for domestic objects such as wooden boxes, spindles, mortars and pestles, baskets and cooking utensils, for which Spanish equivalents already existed. Yet they were displaced by Nahuatl terms.

The evolution of Mexican Spanish suggests something more complex than the usual masculine tale of exploration, of scientific enquiry, of battle and warfare. It is a living reflection of the fact that after the Conquest Amerindian women entered Spanish households as housemaids and wet nurses, but also as mistresses and wives. They raised their *mestizo* children and in doing so ensured the survival of their language and their culture.

It is easier, always, to identify what has happened in human society, rather than to explain why. In the case of Mexico we have many and varied arguments from historians, sociologists, anthropologists and demographers, to explain its rich experience of racial fusion. Some of their suppositions are pragmatic and sensible. It seems entirely plausible, for example, that marriage between Spanish men and indigenous and *mestiza* women was nothing more than a natural response to the shortage of Spanish women in the early years after the Conquest.

The Spanish Crown also played a significant role in fostering *mestizaje*, by providing handsome dowries to young *mestizas*, to enable them to attract Spanish husbands. This system appears to have worked almost too well from the point of view of some colonists. On 6 February 1541, one Jeronimo López took the trouble to write to the King of Spain explaining the predicament of the many Spanish girls and women in the colony who were unable to attract husbands because they, unlike the *mestizas*, lacked vice-regal dowries.

But there are other, more contemplative, arguments. The Brazilian sociologist Gilberto Freyre has argued that Spain and Portugal's eight-hundred-year exposure to Islamic civilisation made its people less instinctively racist than other Europeans whose first experience of dark skin was often in the dehumanising context of slavery.

Or is it possible, as some scholars have argued, that the answer lies in the nature of sixteenth-century Catholicism? It is true that the Franciscans and Dominicans who arrived in Mexico in the wake of Cortés came with the utopian words of Thomas More and Erasmus, the great Humanist scholars, ringing in their ears. For better or for worse the friars came to gather their indigenous flocks to them. They were determined to include them in their world, rather than exclude them. This is a markedly different attitude from that of the Pilgrim Fathers and their followers a century later in North America. These new invaders shunned the indigenous peoples they encountered. They built high wooden palisades around their villages because they could see no place for indigenous Americans in their separatist vision of the New World.

Nor could the majority of British colonists who settled in eighteenth and nineteenth-century Australia easily envisage intimate relations with indigenous Australians. White men did cohabit with Aboriginal women, but never in great numbers and those who did were usually fringe-dwellers themselves: sealers, whalers, drovers, convicts. Miscegenation was not a practice approved by polite Anglo-Australian society, and until the 1970s the children of such relationships were often, as we know, taken forcibly from their mothers to be raised in white families.

The Mexican experience of racial intermarriage is unique in the annals of European conquest. Whatever the reasons for it, whether practical or philosophical, whether voluntary or involuntary, it began with Malinche and the other indigenous women who went with her to the Spaniards at Potonchan. It continued at every other town along the way where civic leaders chose to give their daughters, their nieces, their cast-off concubines to the Spaniards.

Whether she would have wished it or not, therefore, *mestizaje* was Malinche's bequest to Mexico. Yet paradoxically it has also become the principal cause of her execration as a traitor.

It was July, and Filomena was leaving Mexico City soon for El Salvador. She would be teaching in a community on the outskirts of the capital. It would be dangerous, but she told me she was determined to go. We sat beneath the enormous draciana tree in the garden of her cousin's pension. She had brought a poem to show me, but first we talked about Mexico, about Octavio Paz and his famous essay about Malinche.

'I'm used to a society where the majority of people are of mixed race,' I told her. 'But Mexico is different.'

'Why?' she asked me.

'Because here the historic symbolism is so powerful and so painful. Because one side represents the conqueror, the other the conquered.'

'One of our greatest philosophers called us the "Cosmic Race",' Filomena said.

I must have looked puzzled.

'His name was Jose Vasconcelos,' she explained. 'He said we were a cosmic race forged in blood and fire, during that one sudden, catastrophic episode, the Conquest.'

I sat there lost in thought, trying to imagine an Australia forged entirely in such circumstances. A society in which almost everyone was descended from Aboriginal women and white invaders, in which a new race had evolved, as it has in Mexico since the Conquest. As we tried to shake off our British political entanglements, would we too repudiate our indigenous ancestresses, the way some Mexicans have repudiated Malinche, because in the early days they had cohabited with British invaders? Would the sons and grandsons of Truganini and the so-called 'drover's boys' consider themselves dishonoured by their mothers and grandmothers? And what of their daughters? Would they understand and sympathise?

'I've been reading Octavio Paz again,' I told Filomena. *The Sons of La Malinche.*'

She nodded.

'I remember how the first time I saw that title I assumed it meant "The Children of La Malinche".'

'Well,' she replied, '*Los Hijos* can be interpreted either as "the children" or "the sons".'

'Yes, so it came as a surprise to find that in this case it means only "the sons".'

'Of course,' she agreed. 'But Malinche's daughters are entirely absent from that particular work. It is, as you know, addressed exclusively to Mexican men.'

We sat in silence for a while.

'Do you consider yourself to be Malinche's daughter?' I asked her.

She thought for some moments before replying.

'Once I would have denied it,' she said. 'I would have felt ashamed of such a connection. But I no longer believe Malinche dishonoured me. I can admit now to being her daughter.'

It was a warm night, but a few drops of rain had begun to fall.

'I thought you might like to hear something of Sor Juana Inez de la Cruz,' Filomena said, opening the worn volume in her lap. 'A little antidote from the seventeenth century.'

I guessed which lines she had chosen. I closed my eyes and listened as she began to read Sor Juana's famous words aloud in her fluted voice.

Ah foolish men, unreasonable
In blaming woman's nature,
Oblivious that your acts incite
The very faults you censure.

Filomena paused. 'It is three hundred years since Sor Juana wrote those words,' she said, closing her book. 'I have no idea if she had ever heard of Malinche, but she seemed to sense what was to come.'

In Mexico City the night the presidential candidate died, I heard Octavio Paz speak. The television anchorman announced his presence with the solemnity due to Mexico's most famous intellectual. In a culture that values poets above all else Paz had been summoned to offer whatever words of consolation he could conjure in relation to the assassination.

The interview was not what I had expected however. It consisted of a transmission of Paz's voice, accompanied by a silhouette of his profile. It reminded me of a distinguished Roman cameo, and as I listened to him speak in burnished Spanish of his sorrow and despair at this assassination that had desolated Mexico with its sudden violence, I remembered the poems of his I had loved, like 'Hymn Among the Ruins' and 'The Broken Water Jar'.

It seemed curious that such an eloquent and passionate poet should be best known for an essay rather than a poem. *The Sons of La Malinche* is a meditation on many things: on language, on history, on the nature of Mexico, on what it means to be Malinche's son. In it Paz noted that the pejorative word *'malinchista'* had recently been coined by the newspapers. What was the problem with Malinche, he asked, that she should inspire such contempt?

It was the symbolism of her life rather than her personal tribulations that Octavio Paz explored in this, his most famous work. He had no interest in the forlorn sequence of events that brought her to Cortés in the first place, but in his elusive, allusive, elegantly sinuous and sometimes contradictory manner, Paz went deep into the heart of the problem with Malinche. 'To the Spaniard,' he wrote, 'dishonour consists in being the son of a woman who voluntarily surrenders herself: a prostitute. To the Mexican it consists in being the fruit of a violation.'

Malinche, Paz said, had become the symbol, the very embodiment of that violation. She had consorted with Cortés and borne a child to him, the first *mestizo*. She had brought forth a new race of sons, but in doing so she had offended their sense of honour. This, Paz believed, was the essence of Malinche's reputation as a traitor. He made no pretence about political treachery. He seemed to sense that this was always an invalid accusation. Malinche was a traitor to her sons because they saw in her the shame of a violated woman.

The violated woman. Writing in the 1950s, Octavio Paz had invoked the same ancient imagery that had once been so important to the fourteenth-century Culua-Mexica. To them the violated woman had symbolised supreme victory over their enemies, but now, if Paz were correct, she had become an emblem of dishonour and defeat for twentieth-century Mexican men, a reminder of their conquest by Spain almost five hundred years earlier.

From the moment it appeared in 1959, *The Sons of La Malinche* was a controversial work. Many of Octavio Paz's peers among the Mexican intelligentsia found it impossible to relinquish their long-held belief in Malinche's political betrayal. Others flatly rejected his portrayal of such a woman as their mother, as well they might since most of them belonged to Mexico's small white elite and few were truly children of *mestizaje*.

Paz's thesis was essentially a more explicit and disturbing variation on the theme the congressman had adopted in his speech a century earlier: Malinche as a Mexican Eve. But whether intentionally or not, in exploring the sexual dimension of Malinche's image as a traitor, Paz revealed for the first time, as no other commentator had dared to do, the atavistic processes that had blackened her name in Mexican society.

As for the violated woman herself, the meaning of her

symbolism in the eyes of Mexican men might have altered from the fourteenth to the twentieth century, but little else had changed. She remained silent, and the question of her own honour and her private anguish was as immaterial to these philosophical discussions as ever.

V

malinche's children

Look once more at the city from La Malinche's point of view. Mexico is littered with the shells and skulls of Spain... But everywhere you look in this great museum of Spain you see living Indians. Where are the conquistadores?

RICHARD RODRIGUEZ, *Days of Obligation: An Argument with my Mexican Father*

Look Once More at the City . . .

On a cloudy Friday I walked to the Museo Nacional de Antropologia for the last time. On the way I paused for a few moments beside the statue of Cuauhtemoc. He had wanted to die honourably in battle or on the sacrifical stone, but instead he was executed like a criminal on the road to Honduras. Now he stands marooned on his pedestal above Mexico City's busiest thoroughfare.

In Coyoacan in 1982, the city council raised a statue to Malinche. It was, in fact, a statue of Malinche, Cortés and their son, Martin. It was intended to acknowledge those parents of Mexico's *mestizaje*, and in poorer sections of the city or in distant Jaltipan far away on the Isthmus, even in Tlaxcala, the statue might have been accepted.

But Coyoacan was no place for such a memorial. Students and intellectuals took to the streets. The statue was greeted with such derision and indignation that finally it had to be removed. Like the statue of Coatlicue, 'Serpent Skirt', it has been hidden ever since, waiting for the tide of political fashion to swing in Malinche's favour.

Beneath the statue of Cuauhtemoc there is an image of Malinche. It is carved into the stone below his feet, in a frieze depicting the famous meeting on the causeway leading into Tenochtitlan. Malinche stands behind Cortés, not between him and Moctezuma, as she invariably was in the indigenous histories of the Conquest, so her placement has been adjusted. But she is there. And no one would dream of defiling beloved Cuauhtemoc's statue, so she is protected by his presence above her.

The main reading room was full when I reached the museum, so I walked through to the larger auditorium and found a quiet table beside the windows. I sat looking out across the trees for some time, distracted, weary. Filomena had left for El Salvador. Her gifts for her sister in Australia were packed carefully away in my luggage. For me she had left a tiny, painted box with a silver medal of Our Lady of Guadalupe inside. I had only a few more days in Mexico City.

I spent some time leafing through Alonso de Molina's famous early Nahuatl–Spanish dictionary, the *Vocabulario de la Lengua Mexicana*. I admired the way the Nahuatl words stretched themselves across the page with the agility of a cat: long and elegant names like *Popocatepetl, Cihuacoatl, Malinalxochitl,* given visual form in Roman letters. I said them aloud and wondered how I might describe Nahuatl to someone who had not heard it. Tender and sonorous, I would say. Or perhaps I would quote from an old prayer to the Virgin of Guadalupe: 'Like breath through a flute . . . like water flowing.'

The usual fate of indigenous languages is to dwindle and die under pressure from the conquerors' language, but Nahuatl is a surprising tongue. It has spread further in Mexico since the Conquest, and is more populous than it was in 1519 when Cortés first arrived at the river mouth at Potonchan.

In 1554 a Dominican monk wrote a letter to the Spanish Crown complaining about his evangelistic rivals, the Franciscans. 'The friars of Saint Francis,' he explained, 'have occupied a land as large as the Mexican using only one language, where more than two hundred languages are necessary.'

The language in question was Nahuatl, and the Dominican's accusation was true. From the moment they set foot on Mexican soil the Franciscans had embraced this language. They learned it with astonishing brilliance and dedication, spreading it far and wide in their teachings. They compiled Nahuatl dictionaries, wrote Nahuatl catechisms and prayer books. Employing the Roman script the Franciscans transformed Nahuatl into a written language. They gave it new life in a new form. But most importantly, they taught the Culua-Mexica survivors of the Conquest to use Nahuatl to record their histories and their beliefs in their own language.

I stood up to return Molina to the bookshelf and noticed a poster on a display board at the end of the room: 'La Malinche, her Parents, her Children' it read. Or was it her 'Sons'? I walked over to take a closer look. The poster was for a symposium that had been held two years earlier in the philosophy department of one of Mexico City's universities but, with its portrait of a beautiful woman wearing an extravagant headdress of bright feathers, it was clearly too good to be discarded.

A woman working in one of the offices along the side of the room came over to where I stood. 'You seem to like this poster,' she said, looking at me curiously.

'Oh yes,' I replied. 'It's beautiful.'

She told me she was an archaeologist working here in the museum. I explained that I had come to Mexico because of Malinche.

'Why, there is another woman here researching Malinche's life,' she said. 'Come, I'll take you to meet her.'

'She's a linguist and anthropologist,' she told me as we set out along the shining corridors. 'Her name is Rosamaria Zuñiga,' she said. 'I think she will be interested to meet you.' It took us some time to locate the departmental secretary, but when we did she explained that the woman we were looking for was away on leave for two weeks. Two weeks! And I would be gone in two days.

As we walked back together toward the library I asked the archaeologist about the symposium advertised on the poster.

'Do you think its title was intended to mean "the sons" or "the children" of Malinche?'

'You've been reading Octavio Paz?' she replied with a wry smile.

I nodded.

'To be honest,' she said, 'I know very little about that symposium.'

By now we were standing once more in front of the poster.

'But I have a feeling,' she said, looking up at it, 'or perhaps it is just my foolish optimism, that this time it meant her children.'

In Carlos Fuentes's novel *The Orange Tree* Malinche's son, Martin Cortés, remembers how his mother used to cradle him in her arms each night. 'That's the only way we saved ourselves from terror,' he says. 'We hugged each other, my mother and I, shivering with fear.' It is a mirror image in words of the tender scene Diego Rivera had painted on the walls of the National Palace: Malinche with her arms wrapped protectively around her small son's body, as he buries his face in her dress.

In 1942 a direct descendant of Martin Cortés, and therefore of Malinche, published a small history of her life. I found it on the shelves of the library. It was a slender, handsomely bound volume. The author had signed his name inside the cover with an elegant flourish: 'Federico Gómez de Orozco'. He had made a gift of his book to the library.

The familiar details of Malinche's life were there: her birth on the Isthmus, her time in Potonchan, her liaison with Cortés. But when I came to the birth of her son, Martin Cortés, I was shocked by what I read. Soon after Martin's birth, Gomez de Orozco had written, Cortés took the infant from Malinche and gave him to his cousin, Luis Altamirano, to raise in his household.

So despite those loving images, on the walls of the National Palace, within the covers of *The Orange Tree,* Malinche may never have cradled Martin in her arms or suckled him, except perhaps during the first few hours of his life, before his father came to take him from her. She was not permitted to raise her child, and if she saw him at all after his birth, it was probably from a distance, until at the age of six he departed for Spain with his father and she lost sight of him forever.

For an Australian like me there was a terrible resonance in this story of a mixed-race child taken from his mother. Orozco had revealed a frightening coincidence of myth and reality in Malinche's legend. If his narrative was correct it meant that when Mexicans claimed to hear Malinche weeping in the night, they were not just commemorating an ancient goddess, but the lamentations of a mortal woman whose child had been taken from her.

Knowing as we do that thousands of indigenous and mixed-race children were stolen from their families in Australia until late into the twentieth century, it is tempting to assume that a similar practice must have been at work in sixteenth-century New Spain. But it was not. Whatever other atrocities sixteenth-century Spain may have condoned, it did not approve of or recommend the removal of mixed-race or indigenous children from their mothers. Such a practice would have contravened both the Church and the Crown's efforts to encourage stability through intermarriage in the colony. However, we know of at least one other notable case of a mixed-race child removed from her mother.

Doña Isabel Moctezuma was around sixteen years old in 1526 when her husband and cousin, Cuauhtemoc, was murdered beside the Candelaria River in the south. She was by then a young and wealthy widow, for the Spanish Crown had recognised her entitlement, as Moctezuma's heir, to many rich estates in what was now New Spain. So on Cortés's return to Mexico City, he married her off to one of his closest associates who died within a few months of their marriage. When her second Spanish husband also died within a short space of time, Cortés arranged a third marriage for her with yet another of his friends.

The fate of Doña Isabel's Spanish husbands suggests that Moctezuma's daughter may have had her own ways of dealing with her predicament. But around the time of her third arranged marriage she became pregnant to Cortés himself. She gave birth to a daughter who was baptised Leonor Cortés, although it is possible Doña Isabel gave her a Nahuatl name which is now lost to us. Leonor too was taken from her mother immediately after birth, and given to the Altamirano family who had also raised Malinche's son, Martin. So Malinche was not alone in the sorrow of losing her child.

Malinche's and Doña Isabel's tragedies were deeply personal, however, rather than political. Had these women been involved with ordinary Spaniards they would undoubtedly have raised their children, as the majority of indigenous women did. But Cortés was a man of the highest ambitions, for himself and for his children. His eyes appear to have been firmly set on marriage into the Spanish aristocracy, a goal he eventually achieved. Not even Moctezuma's noble and wealthy daughter could make a suitable wife for him.

A woman like Malinche could have no place within the lofty schemes of such a man. His determined aspirations, his ruthless nature, his apparent devotion to his first-born son, the confluence of all these things mitigated firmly against her. Had the protestors of Coyoacan in 1982 known that Malinche was never more than a surrogate mother to Martin Cortés, they might have reconsidered their self-righteous denunciations of her.

In 1522 when Martin Cortés was born, he was not the first *mestizo* on the American mainland. Somewhere in the south Gonzalo Guerrero lived on with the Mayan wife and children he had refused to abandon, safe for the moment from the turmoil of central Mexico. And since procreation does not wait for battles and wars to subside, we must presume that other infants had also been born to the various Amerindian women the Spaniards collected on their journey to Tenochtitlan. But as the child of Malinche and Cortés, Martin Cortés could not help but be regarded, symbolically if not in fact, as the first *mestizo*.

In the end Martin's life turned out almost as strange and as tragic as his mother's. It was a life of constant exile, lived almost entirely away from his homeland. He was six years old when Cortés took him to Spain, where he spent his childhood and youth. Soon after his arrival he was legitimised by Pope Clement VIII, invested with the Habit of Santiago, and attached to the Spanish Court as an attendant to Prince Phillip.

In 1554 the thirty-two-year-old Martin is known to have travelled to London for Phillip's wedding to Mary Tudor. He must have cut an interesting figure, this young *mestizo* nobleman in Westminster Abbey. On his return to Spain he married and had at least one son, Fernando, whose denunciation for bigamy I had seen in the Archivo General in Mexico City. By 1563 when

Martin Cortés finally returned to his country of birth, Malinche, his mother, had been dead for thirty-five years.

He seems to have been close to his half-brother, the younger, legitimate Martin Cortés, but this filial affection led him into immediate danger on his return. He was implicated in the colony's first short-lived independence movement in which a plan was devised to overthrow the Spanish monarchy and anoint his brother, the young Marquis of the Valley, as the first king of New Spain.

The records of Martin Cortés's trial identify him as the son of Don Hernando Cortés and the Indian Doña Marina. They also note that his torture by water and rope began on 8 January 1568. 'His arms, legs and feet were tied and stretched and several vessels of water were poured into his mouth,' the scribe in attendance wrote. He remarked that the prisoner refused to admit involvement in the plot, in spite of his sufferings. Finally, however, Martin's physical state deteriorated so critically that the torture was halted. Two days later he was sentenced to perpetual exile from the Americas.

The remainder of Martin's life was 'enveloped in shadows', according to his entry in the *Diccionario Porrua*, but it seems he fought for the Spanish Crown in Algeria and Germany and is believed to have died somewhere in the old Islamic stronghold of Granada during one of Spain's last great battles against the Moors. The precise date of his death is unknown.

Malinche's daughter, Maria Xaramillo, lived until 1569 and raised three sons with Luis de Quesada. She would have been aware of her brother's existence, but if they met at all it was probably in secret, because during the few years Martin Cortés spent in Mexico City they belonged to warring political camps.

As the niece by marriage of the viceroy, Maria Xaramillo was a member of the colony's ruling family. Martin, on the other hand, was implicated in the plot to overthrow the viceroy and invest his younger brother, the marquis, as ruler of New Spain. Martin's years in Mexico City were Maria's last, and she died soon after he was sent into exile.

The legal battle Maria Xaramillo commenced in 1542 against her father, Juan Xaramillo, lasted twenty years, and after Xaramillo's death the tenor of the arguments became increasingly antag-onistic. Xaramillo's widow, Beatriz de Andrade, claimed that Xaramillo had lost so much honour and rank when he married Malinche, that his debt to their daughter, Maria, should be considered fulfilled. Beatriz de Andrade referred to Malinche as 'Marina' without the usual respectful title 'Doña', and although she had never known Malinche she accused her of affecting Spanish airs and graces in her speech and in her dress.

In response, Maria Xaramillo called another round of witnesses to defend her mother's reputation. The usual formal questions were asked, the usual stock replies were given, but among them is one brief and unusually personal testimony from a man named Diego de Atempenecatl. His Nahuatl surname suggests that he was not a Spaniard but probably a native of the village of Atempen in the Valley of Mexico.

'I was a servant of the said doña Marina,' Diego de Atem-penecatl said, 'and I was always with her. And I saw that she

TESTIMONY SWORN BY DIEGO DE ATEMPANECATL, C. 1560
(held in Archivo General de Indias, Seville)

always went about in the manner of an honest woman, and in the costume of the indigenous people of this land, and this fact was well known among all the people who knew her.'

'And I was always with her.' Servants were privy to the most intimate secrets of the households in which they laboured. They knew all the infidelities, the births and deaths, the loves and hates. Diego de Atempenecatl could have told us a great deal about Malinche, but we never hear another word from him. His testimony is as concise, as rare and as dignified as that one very personal glimpse he permits us of Malinche.

A few days before leaving Mexico City I went back to the painting beneath the stairs in the old Colegio de San Ildefonso. I sat there in the shadows, looking up at Malinche, and saw in her the perseverance and immensity of those ancient divinities Coatlicue and Cihuacoatl, and of the countless Amerindian women who endured and survived the Conquest. Men may have died honourably in battle or on the sacrificial stone, but women like Malinche faced a different kind of struggle. They were obliged to consort with the enemy, to bring forth children in a devastated world and learn to love them, whatever the bitter circumstances of their conception.

Malinche was not alone in this. There were Moctezuma's daughter, Isabel, and her half-sisters Ana and Marina. There was Luisa de Xicotencatl, the daughter of the lord of Tlaxcala, who spent her entire life with Pedro de Alvarado, a Spaniard whose hair was so golden that the Tlaxcalans nicknamed him *Tonatiuh*, the Sun. There was Elvira de Toznenitzin who married the interpreter Geronimo de Aguilar, and there was Angelina, an otherwise unknown Mayan woman who became the common-law wife of Bernal Diaz and bore him several children. In all but the most illustrious cases, we know very little of these women. Yet like Malinche they and thousands like them were the founders of what the philosopher, Vasconcelos, called the cosmic race of modern Mexico.

The first time I saw Mexico City it was a cool winter's morning in January. The last time was a late summer's night in the midst of a wild electrical storm, the kind Bernal Diaz had described after the fall of Tenochtitlan. At the airport I fell into conversation with an elderly Mexican woman. She was off to see her children and her grandchildren in Los Angeles. She had never flown before, but she sat there calmly in her *huipil* with her best shawl wrapped around her shoulders, her white hair pulled back into a bun at the nape of her neck. She asked me how I liked *la capital*. I told her I was deeply attached to it. '*Sí*,' she nodded gravely, '*es magnífico*.'

I would miss the Great Temple of Huitzilopochtli where Malinche had instructed Moctezuma to tear down his idols and erect a cross. I would miss the Iglesia de Jesus Nazarene, too, where Cortés's bones had finally been laid to rest, and the tiny lizards and hummingbirds in the pension garden. But I was homesick and longed for cold, bright winter skies, for the sigh of wind in the trees, the crash of icy waves on the shores of the Southern Ocean, the haunting cries of foxes in the night.

My plane took off around nine o'clock. As I flew north raindrops glistened against the cabin window. I knew that somewhere among the pools of light twinkling in the towns and cities below was Aztlan, the place of the white-feathered heron, where Malinalxochitl and her fellow Azteca had begun their long journey south toward their destiny in the Valley of Mexico. Aztlan is still there but it goes by another name now: Mexcaltitan. A humble village on an island in a warm estuary beside the Pacific Ocean, a village with one solitary road running around its perimeter.

I had wanted to visit the island in the estuary but I had run out of time and knew I must content myself with the crumpled aerial photograph I kept folded inside my journal. Perhaps it was better that way. From the vantage point of that photograph Aztlan's ancestral relationship to mighty Tenochtitlan was unmistakable: a city on a circular island, in a tranquil lake. Where herons abound.

In Avenida Madero the day before I left Mexico City I had spent my last pesos on a book for the long journey home: *Days of Obligation: An Argument with My Mexican Father* by Richard Rodriguez. I opened it on the plane and began to read. 'I used to stare at the Indian in the mirror,' Rodriguez had written. What he saw reflected in his looking glass was a dark and elongated face that belonged in the pages of *National Geographic* or on a temple frieze in Chichen Itza or Palenque. Rodriguez was raised in Sacramento, California, but he too is a child of what he calls the 'epic marriage' between Mexico and Spain, between Malinche and Cortés.

He described his first visit to Mexico City. How he stood on a busy street corner and everywhere he looked he saw his own countenance. That was when he recognised for the first time the absurdity of Europe's boast that in 1521 Spain had conquered Mexico. 'Where, then,' he asked, 'is the famous conquistador?' Vanished, he concluded, as he stared into the *mestizo* faces around him, vanished, absorbed and diffused by the endurance of Amerindian women.

Richard Rodriguez understands as well as Octavio Paz that Mexico's problem with Malinche is, fundamentally, a question of how to honour a rape. Rodriguez too is Malinche's son. Yet he finds nothing to mourn, no loss of honour to lament, in his *mestizo* status. 'My life began,' he says, 'it did not end, in the sixteenth century.'

His life began with Malinche. With this ancient, scattered jigsaw of a life, a woman's life, cradled like a small cantilena within the great and tragic song we call the Conquest of Mexico.

Timeline

c. 1466   Birth of Moctezuma Xocoyotzin in Tenochtitlan

1485   Birth of Hernan Cortés in Medellin, Spain

1492   First voyage of Christopher Columbus to the Americas (West Indies)

c. 1500   Birth of Malinche in the Isthmus of Tehuantepec, southern Mexico

1502   Moctezuma assumes leadership of Culua-Mexica (Aztecs)

1504   Cortés arrives in West Indies

c. 1510   Malinche sold into slavery among the Maya of Potonchan

1511   Geronimo de Aguilar shipwrecked on Caribbean coast of Mexico

1519   Hernan Cortés departs Cuba on exploratory voyage to American mainland
Rescue of Geronimo de Aguilar
Malinche is given to Cortés by the Maya of Potonchan
Cortés arrives in Tenochtitlan
Death of Moctezuma Xocoyotzin

1520   Spaniards driven from Tenochtitlan (la Noche Triste)
        Cuauhtemoc assumes leadership of Culua-Mexica

1521   Siege and Fall of Tenochtitlan

1522   Birth of Martin Cortés, son of Malinche and
        Hernán Cortés

1524   Malinche and Cortés embark on journey to Honduras
        Malinche marries Juan Xaramillo

1525   Cortés executes Cuauhtemoc

1526   Birth of Maria Xaramillo, daughter of Malinche and
        Juan Xaramillo

1528   Martin Cortés (aged 6) departs for Spain with his father,
        Hernan Cortés
        Last reference to Malinche in council records of
        Temystitan-Mexico

1529–30   Juan Xaramillo remarries to Beatriz de Andrade

1547   Cortés dies in Spain

1584   Bernal Diaz del Castillo dies in Antigua, Guatemala

Glossary of Spelling and Pronunciation

Many of the Spanish names in this book will be familiar to readers, especially that of Hernan Cortés. But sixteenth-century Spanish orthography, like sixteenth-century English, had many variations, especially in relation to personal names and place names. In my own references to Cortés I employ the common twentieth-century version of his name, 'Hernan', but where contemporary sources refer to him as 'Fernando', 'Hernando' or 'Ferdinando' I have left it as such.

Moctezuma's name has known many variations in both Spanish and English, all of them approximations of the sixteenth-century Nahuatl pronunciation. The editor of Cortés's letters, Anthony Pagden, suggests 'Motecuçoma' as probably the most authentic phonetic transciption. I have stayed with 'Moctezuma', the more common Spanish form, simply out of personal habit, but readers should note that in some older English texts he is called 'Montezuma', and that in the Nahuatl text of the Florentine Codex his name is spelled 'Moteucçoma'.

The name Tenochtitlan for Moctezuma's city clearly caused confusion among the Spanish conquistadors. Its spelling has several variations in the contemporary sources such as Cortés's letters and Bernal Diaz's narrative of the Conquest, including 'Temixtitan' and 'Temystitan'.

PRONUNCIATION

'Malinche' is always pronounced 'Mar-leen-cheh'.

'Malintzin' is pronounced 'Mar-leen-tzin'.

'Marina' is pronounced as in English except that the 'r' has
a single trill, as in Scottish 'Robert'.

NAHUATL PRONUNCIATION

'x' is pronounced like English 'sh'; see 'Tlaxcala', 'Malinalxochitl'.

'tl' at the beginning of Nahuatl words is pronounced like 'tl' in 'atlas'.
But in everyday speech at the end of words like 'Popocatepetl'
and 'Nahuatl', the 'l' tends to disappear.

'z' is pronounced 's' as in 'so'; see 'Moctezuma', 'Iztaccihuatl'.

'hua' is pronounced 'wah'; as in 'Cihuacoatl' (See-hua-co-waht).

'ch' in words like Tenochtitlan and Malinche is pronounced
as in English 'church'.

Select Bibliography

BERNAL DIAZ DEL CASTILLO left a great gift to future generations in his *True History of the Conquest of New Spain*. Almost five hundred years after he wrote them, his plain words still express better than any poet or historian has ever done, the wonder he felt as a participant in Spain's momentous invasion of the American mainland. In preparing this book I have used the edition of his *Historia Verdadera de la Conquista de la Nueva España* (prepared by Joaquin Ramirez Cabanas, Mexico City, Editorial Porrua, 1966). A highly readable and abridged English translation edited by J. R. Cohen is also available to those who do not read Spanish (*The Conquest of New Spain*, Penguin, 1963).

HERNAN CORTÉS's *Letters from Mexico* (translated and edited by Anthony Pagden, Yale University Press, 1986) is a fascinating portrait of both the Conquest and the conqueror. So is J. H. Elliott's *The Mental World of Hernan Cortés* (in Transactions of the Royal Historical Society, Fifth Series, 17: 41–58, 1967). In this penetrating and intriguing essay Elliott examines the literature and ideas that inspired Cortés, and explores the famous but erroneous story of the burning of the ships at Veracruz.

THE FLORENTINE CODEX is so called because the original manuscript now resides in the Biblioteca Medicea Laurenziana in Florence. Fr Bernardino de Sahagun, the great Franciscan ethnologist who supervised the manuscript's compilation by young Mexica noblemen, initially entitled this extraordinary work *Historia General de las Cosas de la Nueva España (General History of the Things of New Spain)*. The original *Historia General* was written in Nahuatl with a parallel text in Spanish. Copies of the original, along with editions of the Charles Dibble and Arthur O. Anderson English translation, (Arthur J. O. Anderson and Charles Dibble, Santa Fe, School of American Research and the University of Utah Press, 1950–82), can be found in academic library collections in Australia, Europe and the United States.

Life among the Culua-Mexica of Tenochtitlan prior to the Conquest is explored in great depth and with rare elegance by INGA CLENDINNEN in her definitive work *Aztecs* (Cambridge University Press, 1991). I also recommend her article 'Fierce and Unnatural Cruelty: Cortés and the Conquest of Mexico'. This essay, published in 1991 in edition 33 of the journal *representations*, offers a perceptive and thought-provoking interpretation of the behaviour of Cortés, Moctezuma, Cuauhtemoc and the Culua-Mexica in general during the Conquest.

We People Here: Nahuatl Accounts of the Conquest of Mexico (University of California, Berkeley, 1993) by JAMES LOCKHART offers the most recent English translation of Book 12 of the Florentine Codex, and of lesser-known documents such as the *Anales de Tlatelolco*, which deal specifically with the catastrophic events of the Spanish Conquest from the perspective of the conquered. In his translation of these texts Lockhart reveals that the Culua-Mexica possessed a far more sophisticated understanding of the Conquest than the popular myth of their superstitious fatalism would have us believe.

For insights into the construction of Malinche's legend as a traitor, *Los Hijos de la Malinche* (*The Sons of La Malinche*, in *El Laberinto de la Soledad*, Mexico City, Fondo de Cultura Económica, 1959) by OCTAVIO PAZ and *La Malinche in Mexican Literature: From History to Myth* (University of Texas Press, Austin, 1991) by SANDRA MESSINGER CYPESS, are invaluable and eloquent works. Messinger Cypess's treatise also reveals an emergent body of Malinche-inspired work among Mexican-American [Chicana] poets in Los Angeles and San Francisco.

CECILIA KLEIN's intriguing study of the adoption and development of Cihuacoatl's mythology by the Culua-Mexica is entitled 'Rethinking Cihuacoatl: Aztec Political Imagery of the Conquered Woman'. It is found in volume 1 of *Smoke and Mist: Meso-American Studies in Memory of Thelma D. Sullivan*, edited by J. Kathryn Josserand and Karen Dakin, British Archeological Reports, Oxford, 1988.

RICHARD RODRIGUEZ's *Days of Obligation: An Argument with My Mexican Father* (Penguin, New York, 1993) is too deeply complex a work to be easily categorised, but among its riches is a thought-provoking exploration of what it means to be a son of Malinche. Rodriguez offers an alternative response to the earlier one of Octavio Paz in *Los Hijos de la Malinche* (*The Sons of La Malinche*).

Many participants in the Conquest of the Culua-Mexica left sworn affidavits or *probanzas* of their deeds in order to claim land, riches, titles or other benefits from the Spanish Crown. This is true of Malinche's husband Juan Xaramillo de Salvatierra, her former co-interpreter Geronimo de Aguilar, Bernal Diaz del Castillo, and Doña

Isabel Moctezuma and her sisters. *Probanzas* were also initiated by children and grandchildren of deceased conquistadors. In 1542 Malinche's daughter and son-in-law, Maria Xaramillo and Luis de Quesada, compiled a *probanza* in Malinche's name as part of their legal action against Juan Xaramillo, and in later years Malinche's grandsons Pedro de Quesada and Fernando Cortés also instituted *probanzas* in her name for their own purposes.

Virtually all those who marched with Cortés and later, with Francisco Pizarro in Peru, compiled and swore such *probanzas* as they sought compensation from the Spanish Crown for their efforts during the conquests in which they participated. The majority of these documents are held in the Archivo General de Indias in Seville. They are a rich source of biographic material for those interested in the extraordinary and tragic era of sixteenth-century Spanish imperial expansion in the Americas.

Index